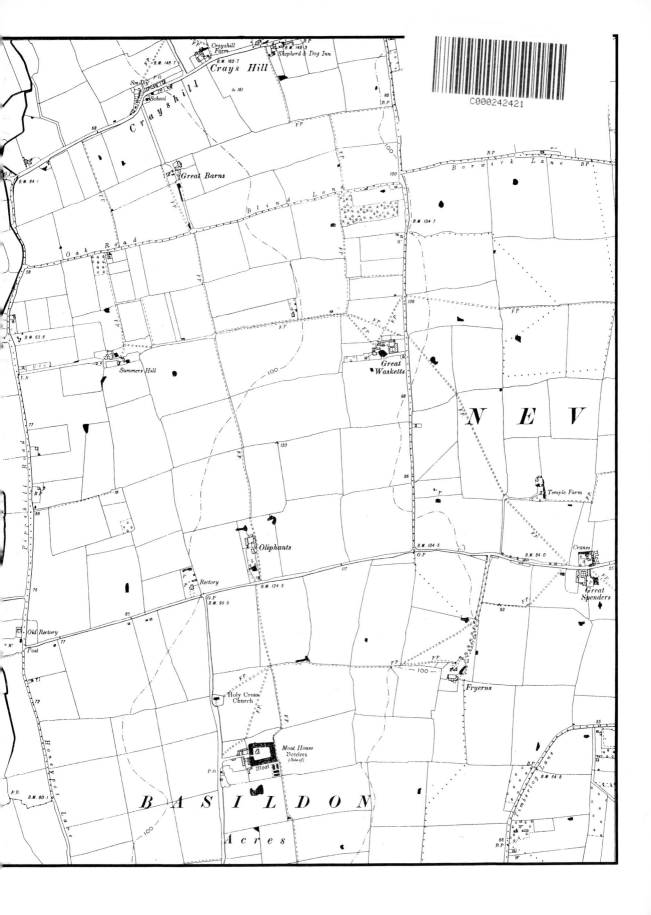

BASILDON

Endpapers:
Ordnance Survey maps of Basildon district in 1898 show the agricultural nature of the area at the time. The Laindon map (*front endpaper, left*) shows four farms in Wash Road only two of which survive today. Hunt's Farm and Brewitt's Farm can also be seen — they stood on land now occupied by the town's Gloucester Park.

Virtually the only remaining landmarks still standing in Basildon (*front endpaper, right*) are Holy Cross church and Great Wasketts Farm at Nevendon. However, the Basildon map includes names like Botelers, Great Spenders, Cranes and Fryerns which were used by the New Town developers for roads or housing areas.

The Vange (*back endpapers, left*) and Pitsea (*back endpapers, right*) maps show the two railway lines from London which converge on Pitsea, one via Laindon and the other via Tilbury.

South of the Tilbury line can be seen the site of the old brickworks at Vange while the same map shows several old homes like Basildon Hall and Vange Hall, both sacrificed for the redevelopment of the area.

The Pitsea map shows one of the few old buildings to survive the creation of the New Town — Pitsea Hall near Pitsea station. It also shows the munitions factory site on the marshes, now largely occupied by the Wat Tyler Country Park.

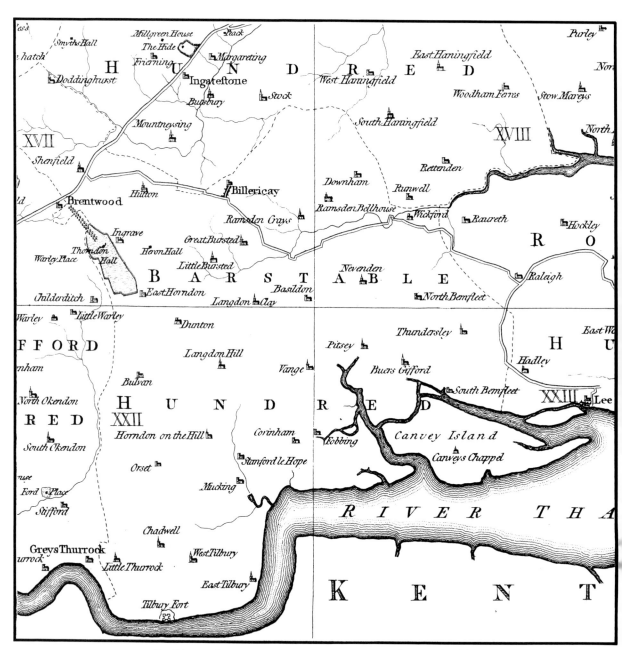

Basildon and area from the Chapman and André map of 1777.

BASILDON

Peter Lucas

Phillimore

1991

Published by
PHILLIMORE & CO. LTD.
Shopwyke Hall, Chichester, Sussex

© Peter Lucas, 1991

ISBN 0 85033 749 6

Printed and bound in Great Britain by
STAPLES PRINTERS ROCHESTER

Dedicated to Pam
1931-1990

Contents

	List of Illustrations	ix
	Acknowledgements	xii
1.	Putting Basildon on the Map	1
2.	The Plotlanders	10
3.	Before the New Town	22
4.	The War Years	38
5.	The Creation of the New Town	48
6.	The New Town Pioneers	53
7.	Basildon: the Ups and Downs	66
8.	The Newcomers' Greatest Needs	77
9.	Councils, M.P.s and Elections	91
10.	Civic Offices and Council Officers	102
11.	Basildon Development Corporation	108
12.	Royal and Famous Visitors	113
	Index	119

List of Illustrations

1.	H.E. Bebington, estate agent's offices, Langdon Hills	3
2.	Fairview estate from Vange railway line	4
3.	Steam train approaching Laindon station	4
4.	Summer scene in old Basildon	5
5.	Basildon-Laindon-Pitsea area, early 1930s	6/7
6.	Simmonds family, Dunton Hills Estate	11
7.	Plotlanders at their weekend homes, Laindon	11
8.	Burke family at Dunton plotlands	11
9-13.	Various types of homes on the plotlands	12/13
14.	Carey Brothers' yard, High Road, Laindon	16
15.	A pre-war Laindon road	16
16.	Nightingale Parade, High Road, Langdon Hills	18
17.	Alec Street's shop, Station Lane, Pitsea	18
18.	Post Office, Langdon Hills	19
19.	High Road, Vange, post World War Two	19
20.	'The Haven', Third Avenue, Dunton	20
21.	Junction of Station Lane and London Road, Pitsea	22
22.	Mr. H.G. Howard and the Pitsea Band	23
23.	St Alban's church hall, Church Road, Basildon	25
24.	Church Road and Rectory Road junction, Basildon	25
25.	*Fortune of War* on the Arterial Road, Laindon	27
26.	Ted Short, R.A.C. patrolman	27
27.	*Daily Telegraph* article on Vange firemen	28
28.	Vange firemen	28
29.	High Road, Laindon, in the 1920s	31
30.	Dr. William Shannon	31
31.	Basildon's old Rectory	32
32.	Dick Hillman's Daimler taxi	34
33.	Old Tom's early buses	34
34.	Matron's house, Langdon Hills Sanatorium	36
35.	The Rutters at the sanatorium	37
36.	Nurse Iris Gower	37
37.	Air raid wardens and civil defence personnel	39
38.	Bomb damage at the Rectory, formerly Oliphants, 1940	40
39 & 40.	Wrecked homes in Gordon Road and Fairview Road, Basildon, 1944	42
41.	Ted Wright with the Chamberlain emblem, 1940	43
42 & 43.	Wrecked homes on the Dunton Hills estate, 1940	44
44.	Nevendon's Dad's Army, 1940s	45
45.	Laindon Home Guard	46
46.	A break in training for the Laindon Home Guard	46
47.	Aerial view of old Basildon village, 1954	49

48.	Mrs. Betty Walker, 1951	53
49.	Barstable area, 1948	55
50.	Councillor Alf Dove	57
51.	Chairman Alf Dove, 1963/4	57
52.	Methodists' 'church', Nelson Road, Basildon	60
53.	Holy Cross church, Church Road, Basildon	62
54.	Ordination service, St Martin's church, Basildon	62
55.	Mr. John Moyler	64
56.	Old and new Vange	67
57.	Ghyllgrove estate	67
58.	Early New Town housing, Holden Gardens, Fryerns	68
59.	Old age pensioners' bungalows, Fryerns estate	68
60.	The Allan family, Luncies Farmhouse	70
61.	Cranes Farmhouse, Basildon	71
62.	'Oliphants', off the old Rectory Road	71
63.	Chalvedon Hall, Pitsea	71
64.	Pitsea Hall	73
65.	Barstable Cottage, Basildon	74
66.	The James family at Barstable Cottage	74
67.	Shopping parade, Whitmore Way, Fryerns	78
68.	Shops, Keay House block, 1959	78
69.	Town centre, 1960	79
70.	Basildon bus terminus, 1961	79
71.	East Square, Basildon, 1961	80
72.	Aerial view of Basildon General Hospital, 1973	82
73.	Swan Mead Junior school, Vange, recorder group, 1964	84
74.	Staff at Craylands School, Timberlog Lane, c.1951	85
75.	Laindon School's football team, 1946/7	85
76.	Aerial view showing the development of Gloucester Park, 1957	88
77.	Councillor Harry Tanswell, 1953	92
78.	Mrs. Christina Gadsdon and other Chairmen, 1961	93
79.	Councillor Joe Morgan and Geraldine Gahan, carnival queen	94
80.	Town Manager and Public Relations Officer	94
81.	Councillor John Potter	95
82.	Bernard Braine, M.P., 1953	98
83.	Mr. Edward Gardner Q.C., Sir Alec Douglas Home and Council Chairman	99
84.	Mr. Eric Moonman	99
85.	General election count, 1959	101
86.	Civic function, 1954	102
87.	Town Manager, Robin Mitchinson	105
88.	Public protest against toxic waste dumping at Pitsea, 1977	105
89.	South-East Essex Wholesale Dairies Ltd. factory	110
90.	Carreras Rothmans factory	110
91.	Basildon Development Corporation board, 1986	111
92.	Finnish visit to Basildon housing estate	111

93.   The Duchess of Gloucester's visit to Basildon, 1957   114
94.   The Queen Mother and Sir Billy Butlin   114
95.   The Duchess of Kent in Basildon, 1968   115
96.   Mr. Adrian Huxley-Jones, sculptor   115
97.   Johnny Webb, Olympic walker   116
98.   Alison Drake, Olympic diver, 1973   116

Acknowledgements

The author would like to thank the following for providing material, information or photographs, during the research for this book: Basildon Council Public Relations Office, Basildon Development Corporation Plotlands Album, *Billericay & Wickford Gazette*, Mr. F. Church, Commission for New Towns, Mr. Leslie Eggleton, Essex Records Office, *Evening Echo* Newspaper, Mrs. Chris Hickey, the Land Speculation & Urban Development Study, Mr. David Macintyre, Mr. Tony Moss, Mrs. Joyce Norris, Ordnance Survey Office.

Chapter 1

Putting Basildon on the Map

Basildon of today, with its still-growing population of some hundred thousand people, is a far cry from the tiny hamlet of 179 mainly farming folk who lived there 100 years ago. It certainly bears no resemblance to the settlement of farms, smallholdings, and woodland which existed when Domesday Book was compiled in 1086. Two significant happenings have mainly been responsible for such a dramatic transformation: the construction of the railway lines between London and Southend from 1851 onwards and the selection of the district as the site for a New Town in 1949.

The first railway line, built between 1851 and 1854, hardly affected Basildon or south-east Essex at all. It started from Fenchurch Street, London, and followed a route along the north bank of the River Thames via Tilbury before cutting inland and skirting Pitsea *en route* to the coast. The construction of the line was almost a panic measure by the London, Tilbury and Southend Railway Company (L.T.S.R.C.), which feared losing out to an opposition line south of the Thames that threatened to cream off the passenger traffic from the Thames pleasure steamers. Over the following 20 years this first railway line was of little benefit to Essex for a number of reasons, one of which was that it was very badly managed. It was also handicapped by having only a single track, poor rolling stock and no direct access to a major London terminal.

In the 1870s when interest in railway development was revived it was for a vastly different reason — a new demand for transportation to the coast from the working population of north and east London. Pressure was put on parliament and in 1882 the L.T.S.R.C. was allowed under an Act of Parliament to go ahead with the construction of a direct line to Southend via Laindon and Pitsea. Not only did this line reduce the distance by rail from London to the Essex coast from 43 to 35 miles, but it also opened up huge areas of Essex, including Basildon, which had previously been rural backwaters due to poor communications.

The completion of the new line in 1889, including the building of stations at Laindon and Pitsea, and the effect of the government's Bank Holiday Act of 1871 which gave people more freedom to embark on excursions, opened up the Basildon area. For the first time it came within reach of hundreds of Londoners, who suddenly discovered that they could get away from the capital for a day in the country or at the seaside. Lots of these working-class people had never had a day out before, and for many the possibility of a seaside holiday which Southend could offer was a completely new experience.

In addition to the railways to Southend via Tilbury and Laindon, a second railway company, the Great Eastern Railway, received permission at this time to build another line to Southend via Shenfield. It was a branch line of their main East Anglia line, which had been in existence for some time. With both rail companies opening up links to other London suburban stations, competition for passengers became fierce, leading to both improved services for travellers and considerable undercutting on fares.

Now Southend was only 50 minutes away by rail from central London, the coastal towns and the other districts *en route* were accessible as never before. This led to an unprecedented flow of family traffic, particularly at weekends. Passengers were also greatly encouraged by cheap fares. In 1892 the average cost in England of a second-class single rail ticket was about one penny a mile. By comparison, south-east Essex fares worked out at only $\frac{1}{2}$d. a mile, while excursion and season tickets were even cheaper.

With so much travel activity being created in Essex, it did not take long for the railway companies and land speculators to realise that by co-operation they stood to gain handsomely from each other's actions. On the one hand the railways wanted population growth to boost their all-year-round traffic, while on the other hand the land speculators wanted good rail links to bring people to Essex to live, or just to buy land.

The availability of so much land for sale at that time was caused by the depressed state of agriculture, largely the result of importation of cheap American wheat. Basildon — a name of Saxon origin meaning Beorhtel's Hill — was little different to the rest of Essex in that since the 1870s land had been going out of cultivation. It was not until the drain away from the land had been going on for twenty years or so, however, that the problem was first recognised as serious. In the Basildon district the situation was made worse by the poor quality of the soil: London Clay which held water in wet conditions and became rock hard and cracked in the summer. The cultivation of crops had never been easy here, and when a series of poor harvests occurred in the late 1870s and early 1880s, many farmers were forced to find alternative ways of making a living.

The virtual collapse of the farming industry in south-east Essex warranted a special report by an Assistant Commissioner in 1893. The area selected for his study covered 223,000 acres between the River Thames and the River Blackwater, and stretched as far as Billericay and Stanford-le-Hope in the west. When his report was published it disclosed that about thirteen per cent of all farming land in the study area — over 28,000 acres — had passed out of cultivation between 1880 and 1893. It also stated that the trend away from farming was likely to continue, and if so there was little likelihood of the land ever being returned to agriculture. The commissioner expressed the view that because of the London Clay soil the fields would soon degenerate into coarse weedy pasture colonised by low scrub vegetation of the kind so familiar in Basildon later.

In the 1890s farmers had very limited technical knowledge and those who made a brave effort to get the land under control again were mainly unsuccessful. Faced with the high capital costs of land recovery solutions suggested to them, many farmers discovered through contact with land agents that greater profits could be achieved by selling off their land for building. As a result, many took the easy option and gave up all notions of ever farming again. Those who sold their land to the agents or to other landowners took the money and moved on to other activities. It then became the responsibility of the agents to sell the land.

Possibly the largest agent operating in Essex was the Land Company, of London, formed in 1880. Its object was to purchase or hold on behalf of clients most of the potential building land in south-east Essex, including Basildon and Canvey Island. The company also had similar interests in Kent, the Isle of Sheppey and other parts of the Home Counties. Basildon also had its own land agents, including Harry Foulger and Thomas Helmore at Laindon and Robert Varty and James Humm at Pitsea. Frequently they acted on behalf of the larger agents and also for local builders.

1. Estate agents involved in the plotland sales usually had tiny offices like this one in High Road, Langdon Hills, belonging to H.E. Bebington. Most of the offices were close to the railway stations.

The land speculators at this time all worked to very similar systems, drawing up plans showing plots and roads before offering a particular area for sale. Often they attempted to prevent land prices falling to ridiculous levels by placing a minimum price on each plot, which were on average 18 ft. wide. They also released only a small amount of land at any one time.

Land prices in this period were generally low in most parts of the country and it was necessary to offer various incentives to attract prospective buyers to sales in Essex. Auctions were normally held on the estates between April and October, and these were widely advertised in suburban newspapers and at London railway stations. The railway companies usually ran special cheap-fare trains to and from London for the sales. Should a ticket holder purchase a plot, the difference in cost between the cheap fare and standard fare was often paid as commission to the railway by the land agents. Free

2. A view from the railway line at Vange of the Fairview estate, west of Timberlog Lane.

3. A steam train approaching Laindon station from Dunton, showing plotland homes in the Helmore Crescent area of Laindon.

4. A typical scene in the Basildon area in the summer months — scattered development reached by grass tracks.

lunches and champagne were also provided on some occasions, a policy which often attracted people to the sales for the wrong reason. Free transport to and from the stations was always provided even by the smallest agents. In addition to the cheap fares and free liquor, the land agents organised competitions and sometimes gave away plots of land as prizes. Even the railways joined in the spirit of the sales, offering free season tickets for purchasers of plots. The end result was that for both the speculators and the railway companies south-east Essex became a goldmine and both made fat profits from their operations.

As far as Basildon was concerned, the ruthless selling tactics used by speculators were aimed principally at three elements of the London population. First, they thought the cheapest land furthest away from the railway stations would attract retired people who no longer required regular access to London. Second, they foresaw the areas around the stations of Laindon and Pitsea utilised mainly by London workers for week-end or summer retreats. Third, over the whole of south-east Essex, company managers and

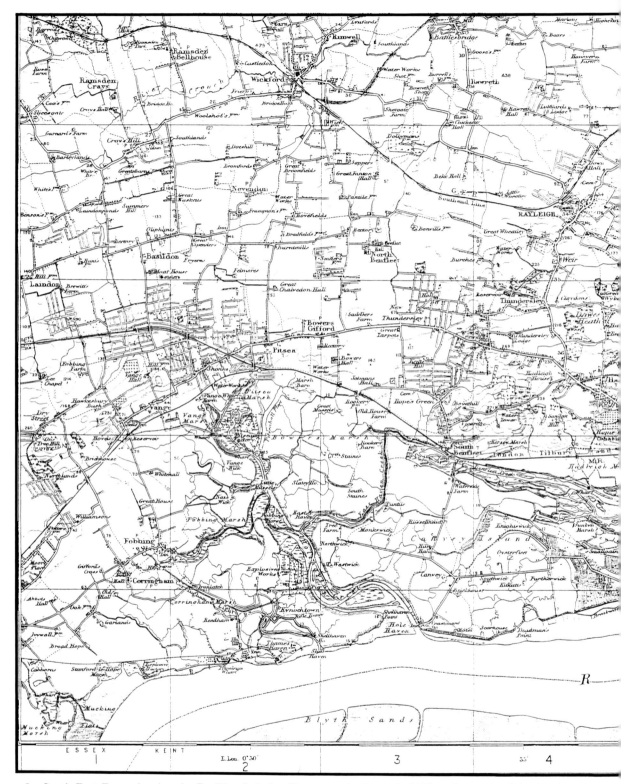

5.   South-East Essex showing the Basildon-Laindon-Pitsea area in the early 1930s, when most of the development was near Laindon and Pitsea stations.

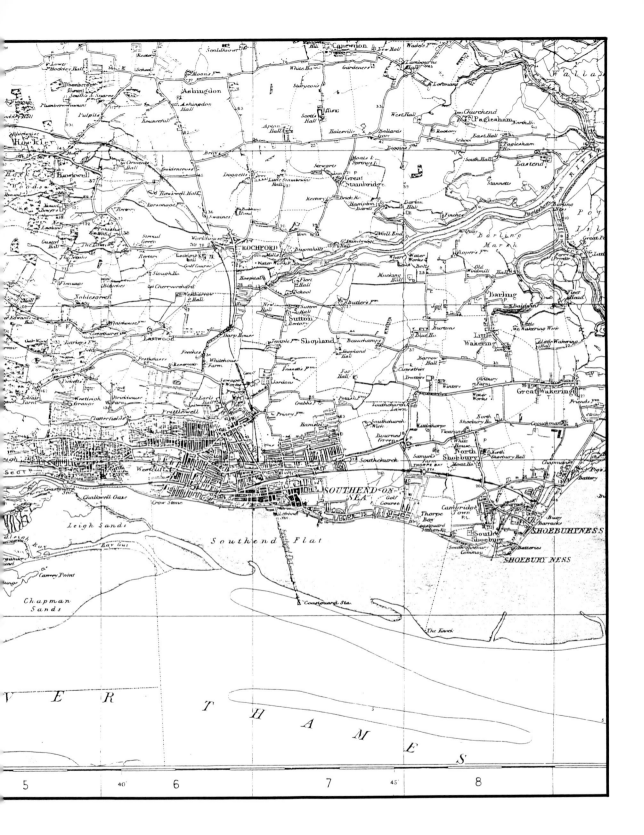

white-collar workers were encouraged to live in the area and to use the railway to commute to work in the City.

Most of the Basildon area land was offered for sale between 1885 and 1910. Supply exceeded demand, however, and many of the plots were not sold until the years between the two world wars, which saw the greatest influx of people into the district, mainly from the suburbs of London. The first sites to be sold were usually those close to the stations, but as the villages expanded, plots were bought and developed in an ever-widening circle around them. Large tracts of land two miles or more from the stations were never sold and much of it was returned temporarily to agriculture or related uses during the Second World War. Most plots were bought for week-end use by people wanting to escape from the noise and grime of London. Hundreds of them, however, remained unused and overgrown, while others were developed with a variety of structures ranging from buildings of very flimsy wooden or asbestos construction to solid brick-built homes.

The more well-off people were attracted to good quality houses built along the main roads, like London Road at Pitsea and Vange and the High Road at Laindon and Langdon Hills, by local builders in association with the land agents. At Pitsea in the 1920s a building firm called Boyce Brothers advertised 'substantially built brick bungalows' for £395 each. Loan repayments over 20 years worked out at a little over 10s. a week.

With so much land on offer, some agents became involved in other money-making schemes. One was a plan promoted in the 1890s for 'a recreational suburb for London' to be built close to Laindon Station. Although the developers, the Land Company of London, neither owned the land nor had any previous interest in recreational development, they proposed to construct a racetrack with a 2,000-seat grandstand — a replica of one at Sandown Park. Also involved in the plan was a golf course, parks and sports facilities as well as an estate of 'good quality' homes. The scheme failed to get beyond the catalogue stage and the site around the *Laindon Hotel* went on to become yet another area of low-standard housing like that in so many other parts of the district.

A 1970s urban studies paper on urban development and land speculation stated that between 1890 and 1910 some fifty to sixty thousand acres of land were offered for sale in south-east Essex. This was totally unrelated to the demand for it. Except in a few choice locations it was impossible at many sales to reach anywhere near the reserve price for a plot. Sometimes it was even difficult to give the land away. The reason was that many of the people taken to the sales by the land agents could never afford to build on the land or even to pay the rail fare to reach the plots regularly.

Some who did buy left the land undeveloped and as owners died title deeds were lost; many heirs never even realised that they owned pieces of potentially valuable land. A great number of these owners have never been traced to this day. The problem was inherited by Basildon Development Corporation in 1949 with its mandate to bring order to an area of planning chaos. Its staff spent many hours in the next few decades attempting to trace ownerships, but in the end it was only the use of compulsory purchase powers that enabled progress to be made on the redevelopment and the creation of Basildon New Town, as it is known today.

Census statistics for the Basildon area from 1801 show that before the arrival of the New Town had such an impact on the figures, the period of greatest population growth occurred during the plotland boom in the 1920s and 1930s. In 1801 the population of the four parishes of Basildon, Laindon, Pitsea and Vange was a mere 707 people, most being at Laindon (304) and Pitsea (211). Basildon had only 62 residents. By 1851 the population of these villages had increased to 950, and it had grown to 1,813 persons by 1900, when there were only 35 homes in Basildon itself.

In 1899, according to *Kelly's Directory*, Basildon had only two shops — a grocery and drapery store owned by a Mrs. Maggie Smith and a post office run by Arthur Hockley. The local nurseryman was Harry Maycock. At Laindon, the only shopkeeper listed, James Mead, kept a shop at the *Prince of Wales* public house, while the village post office was run by the local blacksmith, Tom Newman. Charles Stock had a grocery and drapery store at Pitsea, where John Willsmer was the baker and Herbert Cook the local postmaster. At Vange there were three grocery shops, run by James Cox, William Highwood and Albert Morgan. Morgan was also the postmaster. Another shopkeeper, trade unknown, was John West, and George Lacey of Luncies Road was the local builder.

The main parish churches in the New Town area in 1900 were St Nicholas, situated on the hill at Laindon; Holy Cross in Church Road, Basildon; St Michael, overlooking the marshes at Pitsea; and All Saints at Vange, dating from the 11th century. The only mention in Kelly's of another denomination is of a baptist chapel at Laindon.

By 1921 the population of Basildon district stood at 4,489 (Basildon 644, Laindon 1,205, Pitsea 1,129, Vange 1,067, Lee Chapel 141, and Dunton 303), but 10 years later it had risen to 12,968 people. There was no census during the war, but the next, in 1951, showed a figure in excess of 34,000 people. Since then the development of the New Town has had a significant effect on the number of inhabitants, which stood at 48,047 in 1961, 80,254 in 1971 and 94,232 in 1981. This increase, together with the marked expansion of the neighbouring towns of Billericay and Wickford, gave the Basildon district a growth rate unparalleled in Essex this century.

Chapter 2

The Plotlanders

Whether they had bought plots of land simply for week-end use, as an investment or as a site for a permanent home, the actions of the plotlanders who played such a significant role in Basildon's history were very similar. Most were attracted to the area by glowing advertisements and publicity material distributed by the land agents and builders. Much of it emphasised 'the healthy and aesthetic aspects' of the estates; the 'pure and invigorating air' and 'the grand views over the River Thames and the Kentish hills' from places like Langdon Hills. One builder described Pitsea as 'one of the healthiest locations in the South of England' and used the fact that there was no doctor resident in the village to substantiate his claim! Some leaflets and publicity material misled buyers into believing that mains water was readily available on the estates, but many found out later to their cost that this meant a standpipe existed, sometimes up to a mile away.

The Depression in the 1920s and also the General Strike of 1926 had a very serious effect on the amount of money available in people's pockets. Both the sale of the plots and their development were hit because many who had earlier bought the cheap land with every good intention of building a property on it found the cost of doing so out of their reach. For those who did make a start, even the cheapest building materials often had to be purchased in dribs and drabs, while the more expensive items such as bricks could only be obtained a few at a time as money became available. As a result many months, sometimes years, went by before some of the properties reached a habitable stage. Others remained half-built and deserted where people had run out of either money or enthusiasm. Some plotlanders used wood and other materials scrounged from various sources near their homes in London and it was usually brought to their plots on the train at week-ends. It became quite a common site at Laindon and Pitsea to see whole families carting wood, sections of partly-built garden sheds, lawn-mowers and other equipment along the roads from the station and across the fields.

Some people brought tents for shelter from the elements and many of these were left up permanently. Others used a wide variety of structures as sleeping accommodation and for cooking, ranging from derelict railway carriages to old London buses. All were adapted to meet individual needs. For the majority, the fresh air and the novel experience of waking to the dawn chorus far outweighed the inconvenience of living in the middle of a field without any of the services people expect today.

A top priority for people making use of their plots regularly was a screened latrine or a wooden earth closet. With no drainage of any kind, the contents of the buckets were disposed of in trenches or holes dug on the site. Another priority was usually a tool shed to house garden implements such as lawn-mowers, scythes or bagging hooks, so essential to keep the grass under control. This task was almost a full-time job.

Week by week and month by month hundreds of tiny homes sprang up right across the area from Bowers Gifford in the east to Dunton in the west. Most were built by

6. (*Above*) The Simmonds family outside their bell-tent on the Dunton Hills Estate.

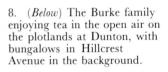

7. (*Left*) The plotlanders had to make their own amusement while building their weekend homes at Laindon.

8. (*Below*) The Burke family enjoying tea in the open air on the plotlands at Dunton, with bungalows in Hillcrest Avenue in the background.

9-13. Various types of homes on the plotlands built mainly of wood with corrugated iron or asbestos roofs. The house shown in plate 13 was constructed from an old railway carriage.

people without any experience of building a chicken shed, let alone a house. Their inexperience showed up clearly in many of the finished products, but in other cases people surprised themselves by producing structures worthy of professional builders. Some were even better and stronger.

Most bungalows were of wooden construction, or made out of asbestos sheets over a timber frame. Today they would be classified as sub-standard, but to the plotlanders they were palaces and their 'little piece of England'. Anyone who called them shacks would soon be put in his place, as the development corporation found later. The majority of the plotlanders made great sacrifices to pay for their land and worked long hours to build their little homes. This explains in some measure why so many fought so energetically to retain them when the arrival of the New Town in 1949 threatened their very existence.

The experience of the Thomas family who lived in an East London flat in 1932, was typical of so many others at the time. It was Mrs. Elizabeth Thomas — mother of a boy of six, twins of three and a baby of six months — who changed the whole direction of the family's life when by chance she read an advertisement in a London evening newspaper. It announced: 'Freehold ground for sale, 20 ft. x 150 ft. plots. £5'. Although husband Henry was far from enthusiastic, Mrs. Thomas insisted on writing off for a plot although she had no idea how she would pay for it. The only thing clear in her mind was that she planned to use it to get a home in the country for her family.

Mrs. Thomas, who later re-married and became a Mrs. Grainger, wrote in 1976 about her journey to see the plot at Laindon with the estate agent. She recalled he had a supply of old stockings in his car and suggested that she slipped a pair over her shoes to protect them during the walk over the fields to the plot. On the way she told the agent she intended to buy it 'if it is nice and quiet there'. As a Londoner she had no idea just how quiet it would be. Convinced she was making the right decision, Mrs. Thomas actually went further and bought two plots, borrowing £1 from her brother to pay the deposit. Her husband thought she was mad. On arriving home she started to worry about paying for the land, but, when she eventually talked it over with her husband, he realised that the plots could be used for week-end stays in the country, and he agreed to help raise the money.

When they had raised £8 10s., the Thomases bought a large army bell-tent and took it by train to Laindon. It was so heavy that they had to leave it on the platform while Mrs. Thomas went off to borrow a barrow from a shop over a mile away. Wrote Mrs. Thomas:

> We put the tent up and when it was time to go home we used to walk a few yards and then stop and look back to see if it was still there. It was wonderful to think that at last we had something to call our very own.

Later, when she started taking her children to the plot, they bought a second-hand pram for 5s. from a junk shop near the station and used it to ferry the children and other odds and ends to the site. With the help of friends they managed to acquire three single beds and a table, and these were given a home in the tent. This meant that the family could stay the night if necessary.

When it became known in London that they owned a plot of land in the country with a bell-tent on it, several local boys asked if they could go there at week-ends. The

Thomases charged them 10s. for four or five boys and saved the money to buy second-hand bricks and sand for building a shed. In later years they became more ambitious and decided to build their own bungalow. When it was finished they liked it so much that they decided to leave London and live permanently in it.

Kate Dew was only a schoolchild when her mother first took her to Laindon in 1908. She went there for a holiday after a serious illness because Laindon's air was reputed to be very healthy, according to the sales brochures. Kate's mother, Mrs. Lerpiniere, was completely sold on the health aspects of Laindon and decided it was the ideal place for her family to settle. To achieve this ambition she began to buy several plots of land during the 1914-18 war, days when people paid what they could afford in monthly instalments, of usually 10s. or £1. Mrs. Lerpiniere then had an old Millwall bus put on one of the plots and took Kate and her three brothers to live in it.

Kate, who was still living in Basildon at the age of 90, said:

> The rest of the family thought she would never put up with the conditions in the unmade roads and the lack of services and were convinced we would all be back in Greenwich within a few weeks. Mum knew what they were thinking and this made her all the more determined to stick it out and prove them wrong. At times life was hard but she refused to give in.

Kate, who married Charlie Dew at St Nicholas' church, Laindon, had many happy memories of 'the good old days' at Laindon and Dunton where she and Charlie lived. 'What was so nice about Laindon was that we had so much freedom. Even the farmers did not mind if we walked over their land.' Of the pioneering days in the plotlands, she particularly remembered the community spirit among the early settlers and the way many of them used candles in jam jars to find their way at night along the unlit tracks. She also recalled walking with her mother the seven miles to Brentwood to collect her father's dole money. On the return journey her mother would treat herself to a Guinness at a public house at Herongate.

When the boom days of plot activity were in full swing in the '20s and '30s, suppliers of building materials like Carey's in High Road, Laindon, did a roaring trade at week-ends and holiday times. Goods ordered one week from Carey's would be delivered without fail to the plots before the following week-end so that work could start right away when the owners arrived on site. The Collings family of Laindon had another business which provided, and still provides, a service to the area. From their High Road shops they supplied every hardware need from paint, nails and screws, to paraffin. Delivery of heavy commodities along the unmade roads depended a great deal on weather conditions. Horses and carts were usually used, but in the winter months even this means of transport was often impossible. Those who used coal for heating and cooking either had to order their winter's supply for delivery in the summer or be forced to carry it a bag at a time from the coal merchant's yard in little barrows or prams.

Mention was made earlier of the spirit which developed among the plotlanders. Where a problem existed someone would always come up with a solution. It was common for people to pool resources and work in groups — often whole families at a time — to provide such things as the network of footpaths which grew up along the unmade roads. The paths were sometimes made of duckboards, which often became treacherously slippery when wet. Other paths were of more permanent materials such as paving stones or concrete, but these were luxuries and the large majority remained just grass. Often, when more money was needed to buy materials, collection boxes

14. High Road, Laindon, showing Carey Brothers' yard on the left. Today, the new Laindon Community Centre has replaced the shops on the right.

15. A typical pre-war Laindon road, although this one had the luxury of a narrow concrete path constructed by the plotlanders.

made from old cocoa tins were placed on fences for people to pop in a few coins. The money was never stolen. In some roads old tin cans and household rubbish were used to provide a firmer base and these were often covered with cinders.

During the winter months conditions were often appalling underfoot and for those who faced a daily trek along muddy tracks to the station, wellington boots were essential. Shoes for work were carried in a bag. At the station the footwear would be changed and the boots left there all day ready for the walk home at night.

With so much activity in the plotlands in the 1920s, trains from Pitsea and Laindon on Sunday evenings were packed to capacity with Londoners who had either been working or relaxing on their plots or who had spent the day at Southend. A special train known as the 'Sunday Night Special' was introduced from Laindon and when it came out of the siding it was usually greeted with a crowd packed eight deep from one end of the platform to the other.

As more people started to live in their little homes, so a sprawl of shops catering for every requirement spread along London Road at Pitsea and Vange, and the High Roads at Laindon and Langdon Hills. Other small shops also sprung up in various locations near the plotland estates. By the 1930s there were 120 shops of all descriptions at Laindon and Langdon Hills on a one mile stretch from the Arterial Road to Samuel Road. At Pitsea and Vange over 90 shops were trading between the *Railway Hotel* and *The Barge*.

For many people in the backwoods, services such as mains water and electricity took a very long time to materialise although promises were made about the provision of water supplies both by the land agents and the Southend Waterworks Company, which took over that responsibility in 1907. In the interim some householders with the expertise (or the money) dug their own wells. Most were able to hold about two-and-a-half thousand gallons, normally sufficient for a family's week-end use for a year. For additional supplies tanks and barrels were used to trap rainwater which was then used for non-drinking purposes, including baths. Some houses had still not been connected by the time the Development Corporation started acquiring properties in the 1950s. It was only after they had been bought out and transferred to a corporation home that many plotland dwellers discovered the luxury of light at the touch of a switch or water at the turn of a tap. To get it, however, they had to forego the feeling of space and freedom which they cherished at their former homes. A good number were very bitter about that.

Today very little remains of the plotlands. At Pitsea and Vange the backwoods sites have been very heavily developed with private or local authority housing, while at Laindon there is little sign of the estate around Markhams Chase which has been replaced by the Lee Chapel North housing neighbourhood. The only connection with the past at Lee Chapel is that the new estate now houses many of the people dispossessed of their former homes in the vicinity, including a high proportion of elderly persons. Perhaps the only place still existing that resembles the original plotlands is at Bowers Gifford, where a number of the side roads still contain various sub-standard properties.

An impression of the past can also still be found at Dunton, west of Laindon, where, thanks to the foresight of Basildon Development Corporation, a plotland trail still exists. The trail includes a typical plotland home called 'The Haven', in Third Avenue, which has been preserved as a museum. It is well worth a visit. The plotland trail

16. Shops at Nightingale Parade, High Road, Langdon Hills, which served the expanding population in the 1920s and 1930s.

17. Alec Street's shop near the railway bridge in Station Lane, Pitsea, where in the 1930s rail travellers left their bicycles before boarding the trains for work.

18. The old, thatched Post Office at the foot of Crown Hill, Langdon Hills.

19. High Road, Vange, as it looked after the last war, before the landscape was completely changed by the New Town development.

starts in Third Avenue off Lower Dunton Road, which can be reached by turning off at the traffic lights in Westmayne near the A127/Research Centre flyover. The car park at the start of the trail is signposted off Lower Dunton Road.

'The Haven', on the left of Third Avenue, is a fairly typical plotland bungalow and one of the few still remaining on the old Dunton Hills estate. It was built by Frederick Mills in the 1930s and was his family's home for 40 years. Mr. Mills bought three plots

20.   Renovating 'The Haven' in Third Avenue, Dunton, which has been preserved as a museum. It is a typical example of many hundreds of former homes in the area.

at Dunton in 1931 and lived in the shed on the right of the bungalow while it was being built. Like many local householders at the time, the Mills family grew their own vegetables and kept a variety of animals including rabbits, chickens and a goat that helped to keep the grass down. They also kept a flock of geese, which acted as watchdogs.

Past 'The Haven', on the left towards the end of the road before it joins Hillcrest Avenue, formerly stood a bungalow called 'Trees', which was occupied by a Special Police Constable and was the first house on the estate to be connected to the telephone, in 1939. Another 19 years went by before other people were able to have a telephone. Tall conifers marked the boundary of 'Trees' and the horse chestnut tree which was still on the site quite recently was grown from a conker planted by the occupants many years ago.

At the top of Third Avenue stood a property called 'Hawthorne', which was on a large 110 ft. x 209 ft. plot owned by the Burke family until 1983. This was one of the sites on which a bell-tent sheltered the family during their week-end visits to Dunton. There is a home-grown tree on this site also — an oak tree grown from an acorn planted by the Burkes.

A roam along the plotland trail, particularly in the summer, cannot help but revive memories of the past in Dunton, when so much feverish activity, now an important piece of the town's history, took place in this quiet corner of Basildon.

Chapter 3

Before the New Town

21.   The *Railway Hotel* (right) and the Tudor-style shops built by Mr. H.G. Howard at the junction of Station Lane and London Road, Pitsea.

Should one person be singled out for making the bravest attempt to change the Wild West appearance which parts of Pitsea and Laindon had acquired through lack of planning control between the wars, Mr. Harold George Howard would be a chief contender. The dream of this dairy farmer and landowner was to turn Pitsea from a country village into a prosperous and thriving town. He loved the architecture of the Tudor period and drew plans for shops and houses in that style and took steps to turn the drawings into reality. The first building to be constructed was the *Railway Hotel*, built on land which he sold to a brewery on condition that the design of the public house blended in with his Tudor dream. Howard followed this up by building the Broadway shops and cinema (now a bingo hall) on the southern side of the High Street and a shop and office block opposite. Both blocks survived the New Town and are still used today. Examples of Mr. Howard's dream for residential development can also still be seen in Howard Crescent, off Rectory Road, facing the park now carrying his name.

When this land was handed over to Billericay Council in 1951, Mr. Howard disclosed that when he first conceived his Tudor plan idea in 1925 his main aim was to create 'something really special' for Pitsea. At the end of the war in 1945 he said he innocently thought that he would be allowed to continue with his plans and at the same time create more employment for the building industry, but once government thoughts turned towards providing a New Town in the area, planning permission was refused. In his speech at the handover Mr. Howard confessed that he was a frustrated and disappointed man. 'Neither I nor my son will be allowed to complete my dream. It is like an unfinished symphony.' Council Clerk Mr. Alma Hatt replied that Mr. Howard had no reason to be disappointed. He had set a standard in his development at Pitsea which would serve as a challenge to the planners of the New Town to match or surpass.

Mr. Howard played a long and important role in Pitsea's business and social life and was also a generous benefactor to the community. His successful business dealings started in the early 1920s when he arranged to deliver milk to a few friends from his farm at Leigh-on-Sea. Sixty years later Howard's Dairies had grown into a prosperous company, with eight distribution depots, 75,000 customers, 212 retail delivery rounds, 30 shops and 1,000 employees. He and his wife Rose celebrated their golden wedding

22. Mr. H.G. Howard, dairy farmer (centre), with the Pitsea Band he helped to form before the last war.

on 11 March 1961, but three months later he died peacefully at home while watching television. He was buried in the family's enclosure at St Margaret's church, Bowers Gifford, which he loved so much.

In old Basildon village the three main roads were Rectory Road from west to east and Church Road and Timberlog Lane running from north to south. Although now split up into sections, Church Road still exists on much of its old line, while Timberlog Lane — although much reduced in length — still remains between Clay Hill Road and Broadmayne. Rectory Road stretched from approximately the present position of the Festival Hall in Pipps Hill Close to Gardiners Lane near the present York factory. For over 400 years it was an important part of Basildon's history yet when it was obliterated from the map to make way for the Ford tractor plant in 1960, no attempt was made to use the name elsewhere. This was possibly due to likely confusion with the other, equally old-established Rectory Road in Pitsea. The only sections still remaining are the short stretch now known as Gardiners Close and the exit road from the Festival Hall which leads into Cranes Farm Road.

Another old Basildon road which remains, though greatly changed, is Honeypot Lane. In the old days it started at the junction of Pipps Hill Road and Rectory Road approximately where the western end of the Festival Hall stands today. A delightful tree-lined lane, it earned a place in history in 1906 when a middle-aged couple were murdered there. Mr. and Mrs. Watson lived in a tiny shack on the lane and usually obtained water from a pond in their garden. In 1906, however, the pond dried up and they started to use another pond at Sawyer's Farm nearby. For doing this they were murdered by one of two brothers who shot the couple six times at close range. At his trial he said he was angry at someone else taking water from his pond. A news report about the murder stated that if the police had possessed a motor car the brothers might have been arrested on the day of the crime. The report argued: 'This district is such a remote one that a motor car is really necessary and the tragedy suggests the desirability of the Chief Constable being supplied with such means of progression ready for any emergency'.

Before the New Town, the social life of Basildon revolved around the parish church of Holy Cross and its sister church of St Alban's — a wooden building in Church Road near the railway line. As well as a place of worship, St Alban's served as a church hall and was a meeting place for several organisations in the village, including the Women's Institute, British Legion, Boy Scouts and Girl Guides. Later a second church hall was built near the rectory in Rectory Road to serve the needs of people living in the northern end of the village. This hall was never over-used and on some occasions it was brought into use as overnight accommodation in poor weather for parties of scouts or guides camping on the Rectory field. Both halls were demolished during the redevelopment of the town, St Alban's for housing and the Rectory Road hall to make way for the Ford tractor plant.

One of Basildon's best known characters was the village postmaster Bert Holliday, who in addition to running his shop in Church Road also organised many church and other activities. A churchwarden at Holy Cross church, Bert was a forceful character of Scottish birth who was never slow to air his views on any controversial topic either over his shop counter or in his weekly column for the *Laindon Recorder* newspaper, penned under the name of 'Cumbrian in Essex'. Because it upset the rural life of the village

23.   St Alban's church hall in Church Road, Basildon, after a Remembrance Day service. On the far right in the white surplice is Mr. Frank Hall who was the longest-serving lay reader in the Diocese of Chelmsford, between 1912 and 1966. Third from left (also in surplice) was Basildon's village post-master and churchwarden, Bert Holliday.

24.   The junction of Church Road and Rectory Road, Basildon. The tractors and bulldozers are clearing the site to build the Ford Tractor plant. In the distance on the left, behind the 30 m.p.h. sign, is Basildon Parish Hall which was also demolished a few days later as part of the redevelopment.

which he loved, and also the future of his business, Bert Holliday opposed the New Town and lent his support to anyone threatened by it. In the end he too lost his shop and his livelihood, being forced to sell out to make way for part of the Barstable estate south of Fairhouse School. At first the little Post Office and General Stores was used as a temporary police station, but once the constabulary moved to other premises in Basildon town centre it soon disappeared under the bulldozer.

The completion of the Southend Arterial Road in 1925 to provide a direct road link between London and Southend was another milestone in Basildon's pre-war history. As the popularity of motor coaches, or charabancs as they were called, increased, the road became very busy at weekends with day trippers to the coast. It was the same on the A13 through Vange and Pitsea. Most of the charabancs were loaded with ample supplies of beer, but part of the fun for many trippers was to make several stops at public houses on the way to the seaside or during the return journey. The custom led to a number of hostelries, like the *Fortune of War* at Laindon (now the *Hustlers*), the *Harrows* at North Benfleet (now the *Dick Turpin*) and the *Railway Hotel*, Pitsea, being swamped with customers in various states of inebriation demanding quick service during their brief halts. By the time the trippers re-appeared at the public houses on their return journey to London, many were in no condition to remember much at all about their day out. It often led to rowdy scenes and fights which caused annoyance to people living nearby.

The Arterial Road certainly brought new-found prosperity to the publicans who must have been delighted with the building of a second carriageway in 1936. At the same time a roundabout was provided at the Laindon junction, thus relieving R.A.C. patrolman Mr. E. Short of a job. According to the *Laindon and Pitsea Recorder* of March 1936, Mr. Short had been on traffic duty at the junction every weekend for six years without a break. The *Recorder* article also stated that the widening scheme would cost £287,000, although only £66,000 would be spent in the first year.

For many years, until made redundant in the 1950s, Vange's voluntary firemen did an excellent job for the local community. When the alarm sounded, they would down tools at their various places of work and dash off to the fire station near the Working Men's Club in London Road. The morale of the Vange part-timers hit rock bottom, however, in 1936 when their vintage 1912 fire engine was condemned as unroadworthy and ordered off the road by the Ministry of Transport. Determined not to be defeated, the gallant Vange firemen led by Chief Officer Ernie Evelin kept going by using a lorry and private cars to answer emergency calls. The sight of them hooting their way through the streets on the lorry amused some national newspapers and some light-hearted pieces appeared in their columns. One article in the *Daily Sketch* read:

> Imagine the embarrassment of the voluntary fire brigade at Vange (Essex). The firemen say they have been placed in a humiliating position.
>
> When formed six months ago the brigade was provided with a 25 years old fire engine — a converted vehicle which had already been discarded by another station. This has now been condemned and the brigade has to borrow a lorry from a contractor to answer fire calls.
>
> As if this is not humiliating enough, the whole town laughs as they drive to a fire.

The Vange stalwarts were not amused and at one stage threatened to resign en bloc if nothing was done to improve their lot. They rode the storm, however, eventually getting their new engine and going on to provide yeoman service as a back-up to the

25. The *Fortune of War* public house (now the *Hustlers*) on the Arterial Road at Laindon, showing the car park packed with charabancs.

26. R.A.C. patrolman Ted Short on duty at the one-track Arterial Road crossroads at Laindon. Bertie Parkinson's garage is on the left and Modley's sweet shop is on the right.

THIS BRIGADE HAS NO FIRE ENGINE

FROM OUR OWN CORRESPONDENT

SOUTHEND, Friday.

CALLED to a fire at Pitsea, two miles away, to-day, the Vange brigade had to go in two private cars.

When they arrived they found that ladders were needed, so one of the cars had to return

Yesterday the brigade answered a call to a place nearby and had to commandeer a lorry to get there.

You see, their only fire equipment had been condemned by a Ministry of Transport inspector a few days ago. . . .

But the Vange firemen are not amused. Last night they held a fiery meeting and decided to resign if the Billericay Council, the administrative authority, do not promise by Tuesday to provide them with proper equipment.

27. An article in the *Daily Telegraph* on the plight of the Vange firemen after their fire engine had been condemned by the Ministry of Transport.

28. Vange firemen with their old and (right) new engines.

full-time stations at Laindon and Hadleigh before, during and after the war. They were disbanded when the new fire headquarters was built in Basildon town centre, from where all fire operations in the district are now controlled.

For those living in Basildon village in the early part of the century, life was very rural to say the least. One person who moved there at the age of 10 was a young lady who later married into the Chittock family. Clara married Bob Chittock at Holy Cross Church, Basildon, and they continued to live in the area all their lives. They had eight children, six girls and two boys. The couple first met during the First World War while working at Kynoch's munitions factory on the marshes at Coryton, near Stanford-le-Hope. The Chittocks' long association with Basildon was recognised by Basildon Development Corporation which named three roads after the family: Chittock Gate, Chittock Mead and Little Chittock.

One of the Chittock 'girls', Mrs. Joan Keeble, recalled that her mother regularly sent the family's Sunday joint for roasting to Saunders' bakery near the *Barge Inn* at Vange. It cost the princely sum of twopence. Two hours later Mrs. Chittock would send the girls back for the joint, provided with a pudding basin for the dripping. While the Chittock family was growing up there was no resident doctor at Vange, the nearest surgery being at Stanford-le-Hope, but as the population increased a doctor eventually opened a surgery on one day a week in a house near the *Barge*.

*   *   *   *   *

For 34 years a family, which gave its name to Stacey's Corner in Timberlog Lane, served several generations of Basildon people at their little general store. Born in Tottenham, Mrs. Stacey, who eventually survived her husband, was only a year old when her parents brought her to Basildon to live in what is now Luncies Road. She went to school at Vange Primary School and later won a scholarship to Romford County High School. After their marriage the Staceys opened their shop in Timberlog Lane in 1920, when there was little competition of any kind in the vicinity. They had 13 children, but still managed to run a most successful business as well as cultivating a smallholding. The shop was given a new lease of life by the early development of the New Town when it became one of the first ports of call for the pioneering families moving into homes in the Barstable area. It eventually succumbed to the bulldozer in 1954.

*   *   *   *   *

An even longer business association with Basildon was achieved by the Thomas family who ran their garage near the *Barge* at Vange for half a century. It was started by Mr. Edgar Thomas, a Yorkshireman and former Merchant Navy seaman. His sons Archie, Jack and Herbert, and his daughter Emily later joined him to provide a personal, old-fashioned, motor repair service for their many customers in the area. In addition to working in the garage the Thomases were also part-timers with the Vange Fire Brigade for 25 years, seeing service throughout the war and the early days of the New Town. Mr. Edgar Thomas died at the age of 82 in 1959, but his children kept the business going until 1964, when they were forced to sell to the Development Corporation and move to new premises on the Burnt Mills industrial estate.

The Thomases' garage was run on very similar friendly lines to the garages owned by the Parkinsons at Laindon during the same period. The Parkinson garage business first started in Laindon in the 1920s when Mr. Parkinson senior set up in an ex-Army hut in the High Road at the junction of Somerset Road. The garage remained open for over 50 years — Cliff Parkinson keeping it going until the Development Corporation bought him out after a long fight. Cliff then moved to other premises at the corner of Durham Road. Bertie Parkinson's garage was on the Arterial Road at the junction with High Road, Laindon. It was a bigger building than Cliff's, but renowned for the same good service.

*   *   *   *   *

The doctor who pioneered the first medical service in Laindon from 1913 was an Irishman, Dr. William Shannon, who came to the district via northern England, South Wales and London. An army doctor in the First World War, he served in France where he had to treat many horrendous injuries suffered by British soldiers. In 1918 he returned to his home in High Road, Langdon Hills, a large red-brick house just south of the railway line. Having had the experience of working in atrocious conditions in the French trenches, Dr. Shannon was well equipped to tackle the unmade roads of Laindon and Langdon Hills to reach his patients. He became a familiar figure trudging along the muddy roads and across the fields wearing an old mackintosh cape which had seen many years of service.

Dr. Shannon fell from a train on a dark night at Laindon Station and was never the same again. In the last few years of his life he was an invalid but rarely missed the chance of a trip through Laindon's streets in his wheelchair. He died at the age of 76 leaving a widow, two sons and four daughters. On his death the *Laindon Recorder* wrote: 'During his years of service he presented a refreshing figure of informality and disregard for convention'.

The same tribute might also have been applied to another of Laindon's favourite G.P.s, Dr. Dharm Sheel Chowdhary, who served the district for 28 years. Born in the Punjab, 'Doc' Chowdhary came to Laindon in 1931 and became both doctor and friend to many local families. During the Second World War he served in the Civil Defence and the Home Guard and for many years was also the divisional surgeon for Laindon St John's Ambulance Brigade. Dr. Chowdhary died suddenly in 1959 at the age of 59 and his memory is perpetuated in the name of Chowdhary School in Markhams Chase, Laindon.

Possibly the most impressive house in old Basildon village in the early part of the century was the second Basildon rectory in Rectory Road, opposite the junction with Church Road. Last occupied by the rector of Laindon-cum-Basildon, the Rev. Herbert Carpenter, the Rectory was at one time in the early 1900s the only and vital source of water for a number of cottages. The story goes that a Billericay postman who daily walked 16 miles on his round, which included Basildon, regularly pumped up the Rectory's water supply for the incumbent before trudging back to Billericay.

The old rectory, which had replaced an earlier rectory further westwards near Honeypot Lane, became Rectory Farm in the 1930s when 'Oliphants', another old Basildon house nearby, became the official residence of the rector. Although the old

29. High Road, Laindon, in the 1920s, showing Parkinson's Garage, on the right, at the corner of Somerset Road. The *Laindon Hotel* can be seen in the distance.

30. Dr. William Shannon, Laindon's first doctor, who was an invalid for the last few years of his life. He was aged 76 when he died.

31. Basildon's old Rectory which stood opposite the junction of Church Road and Rectory Road. After lying derelict during the last war the Rectory was restored to use in the 1950s as a nursery centre, but then demolished to make way for Ford's Tractor Plant.

building was uninhabited during the war and looked beyond repair, it was brought back into use as a nursery for some years before eventually making way for the Ford Motor Company's tractor factory.

Another local rectory, also now gone, was at Pitsea, and it is in the record books as one of the first houses to get a private water supply, in the district in 1907. This was indeed a luxury at a time when most people in Pitsea had to fetch their water from the Pitsea parish pump at Gun Hill. The pump stood near the entrance to Eversley Road and was the only water supply for miles around until the mains supply was put in.

For many of Basildon's early settlers, the bus services provided by the Campbells of Pitsea and the Websters at Laindon are remembered for their utmost reliability. Apart from an occasional breakdown, the buses kept such good time, mainly with their services to and from the stations at Pitsea and Laindon, that people were even known to set their watches by them.

The Campbell family came to Pitsea in 1890 and their first public service vehicles were horse-drawn. Then during the First World War they converted a lorry into a bus and this became the forerunner of an eventual fleet of 18 vehicles. When Campbells became a private company in 1934, the brothers Dick, Jack and Albert became directors, but all three still drove the buses and were on christian name terms with most of their passengers. Campbells' buses continued to run until 1956 when they sold out to Eastern National, but afterwards the firm continued to run a coach business, mainly for local customers.

At Laindon, early transport from the station was provided in a pony and trap by Mr. Dick Hillman and then by Fred and Sid Hinton who converted a lorry into a bus to transport people to and from the Wash Road area. Later Fred Hinton bought a red London bus, which had solid tyres and an open top deck.

The name which most surviving old Laindoners remember, however, is Old Tom's Motor Services, which was an institution in the town for 15 years. Old Tom's was started in 1921 by Tom Webster with a single Ford charabanc which he himself drove up and down the High Road. Tom painted the name 'Old Tom' on the back of the bus and it became a title which was handed down to every vehicle as the fleet expanded. By the time the business was sold for £8,000 in 1936 to New Empress Saloons, operators of the City bus service, 10 'Old Tom' buses were part of the Laindon scene. Tom Webster and his son Dick, who managed the business from 1931 to 1936, did not give up buses completely and, like the Campbells at Pitsea, continued to run a private hire and excursion business for the local community. For Tom's other son, 'Young Tom', the sale allowed him to branch out as a nurseryman in premises east of the *Prince of Wales* public house in Wash Road, Laindon, next to Benson's Farm. The brown City buses which took over Old Tom's routes operated from Brentwood and were soon to provide a very much expanded service in the area to meet the growing demand.

At peak periods the approach road to Laindon station was often crowded with buses awaiting the arrival of trains. In between journeys the crews spent their time in the wooden Station Cafe drinking tea or playing cards. During the war, for the first time, women joined the crews as conductresses on the buses.

Laindon, Pitsea and Vange were also served in the 1930s and 1940s by two popular long distance bus services — the 2a Westcliff buses from Southend to Romford, and Eastern National's Clacton to Tilbury Ferry service. The 2a double deckers ran through Pitsea and Vange and then along Timberlog Lane and the Arterial Road to Laindon, Upminster, Hornchurch and Romford. They were used a great deal by people going to Romford market or cinemas at Upminster, Hornchurch, Hadleigh or Southend. The Tilbury Ferry buses ran hourly and were used by Laindon children who went to school in Grays or Chelmsford. Even during the air raids in the war, when bomb damage sometimes caused problems en route, the service carried on with few interruptions.

Just before the war one of the Tilbury Ferry buses skidded off the road in High Road, Laindon, and crashed into a large elm tree 200 yards from Dunton Road. A number of bus passengers and the driver were injured and people came out of their houses to give first aid or provide cups of tea for them. The injured were treated in front gardens while they waited to go to hospital. For many hours after the crash the scene in the High Road — approximately where a new roundabout was built to serve Steeple View in 1988 — was one of devastation before the badly damaged bus was towed away. The tree survived and for many years afterwards carried the scars of the impact.

Locally made bread was something which was often taken for granted in old Basildon with family bakers like the Saunderses at Vange and the Cottises at Laindon being always ready to meet customers' needs. Both businesses became established through their reliability and good service, which included daily deliveries to homes even in the most outlying parts of the district. Conditions in winter were often so bad that even ponies and carts were unable to cope with the unmade roads. The roundsmen then had to trudge to their customers on foot, carrying their wicker baskets piled high with bread

32. Dick Hillman originally ran a pony and trap transport service from Laindon station, but later operated a taxi business using this Daimler car.

33. Two of Old Tom's early buses which provided such a valuable transport service for the people of Laindon.

and cakes. Possibly Basildon's most famous baker of those years was 'Doughy' Saunders of Vange who, while he was building up his business, not only baked the bread and served in the shop, but did some of the deliveries too. 'Doughy' also did his bit for charity and his rosy face and rotund figure could regularly be seen in a John Bull outfit leading a Carnival procession on horseback. He was killed in October 1956 by a train as he crossed the railway line at Vange. His business was continued by his son Tom until the premises were bought by the Development Corporation in 1963.

In Laindon the Cottis bakery started later than its Vange counterpart, the High Street shop being situated almost opposite the *Laindon Hotel*, and a second shop in High Road, Langdon Hills. Cottis's was also served by conscientious staff who never failed to deliver the bread, often in spite of atrocious weather conditions. One of the most popular delivery men was Albert Strutt, who became a friend to many of his customers. Albert would do anything on his round for elderly people and it was not unusual for him to chop firewood, fetch a bucket of coal, mend a fuse or change a light bulb.

Other food memories recalled include the delicious pork sausages made by Mr. Perou at his butcher's shop in Bull Road, Vange. They were a particular favourite with Mr. F. Armfield who now lives in Benfleet. Another wartime treat for Mr. Armfield was to have tea and cakes at Jess Keir's cafe, which used to stand opposite Blue House Farm at Pitsea, where Howard's Park is today. To raise money to pay for the teas Mr. Armfield and his friends used to catch and sell rabbits. With meat strictly rationed, they were never short of customers.

There were no local hospital facilities before or after the war, and patients had either to go to St Andrew's Hospital at Billericay, or to Southend for outpatients' services. Clinics did exist at Pitsea and Laindon, but they were small and ill-equipped, and most people relied on their doctors to deal with minor ailments and injuries.

One health facility which was available was a sanatorium for children suffering from tuberculosis. This was tucked away on a beautiful countryside site off Dry Street at Langdon Hills, and it was home for about forty children, mainly from London. The 100-acre site, 278 feet above sea level, including a large farmhouse, was purchased for the sanatorium by West Ham Council in 1927 at a cost of £12,800.

In the 1920s tuberculosis was a killer illness. In fact the *Stratford Express* of 29 October 1927 stated that over 37,000 people died from it in 1926. A further 80,000 cases were notified. The newspaper described the Langdon Hills sanatorium, opened by the Mayor of West Ham, Alderman Ernest Reed, on 26 October 1937, as 'another link in the chain of health services provided for children by West Ham. It commands fine views across the Thames valley and when the weather is fine the river estuary and Southend pier a dozen miles away can be plainly seen'. According to the *Express*, other sites in Harold Wood and Theydon Bois were inspected before West Ham's attention turned to Langdon Hills. Originally the council had wanted 'Goldsmith's', a large house on South Hill, but during the delay in obtaining the necessary consents, another buyer got in first.

The sanatorium was intended to cater for 40 children up to the age of 16. It was built on one level and constructed in such a way as to give patients maximum air and sunlight. In addition to the bedrooms, there was a schoolroom, a dining room, an administrative block and maids' quarters. The farmhouse was adapted to provide quarters for the matron and the nursing sisters.

Today the old sanatorium buildings still exist but are now used as kennels for

34. The Matron's house at Langdon Hills Sanatorium in Dry Street which was used for children suffering from tuberculosis.

boarding dogs. This change of use came as a shock to Mrs. Chris Hickey of Oakville, Ontario, who arrived in Langdon Hills in 1988 looking for the sanatorium in which she had spent five years as a patient during the last war. On holiday in England, Mrs. Hickey visited the site in Dry Street, and when being driven up the driveway became quite excited when she saw the old air raid shelter used by the children during the Blitz still there. Without hesitation she went straight to her old room and found it occupied by an alsatian dog!

Chris Hickey was only seven when she was first at the sanatorium, but she particularly remembers 'the beautiful gardens kept by the four gardeners, which in the spring were full of colour with bluebells, violets and primroses'. Of her stay at Langdon Hills she said:

> Every Saturday we were made to write home. Those unable to write themselves were helped by the nurses who had to show matron all the letters before they were sealed up and sent. After the letter writing we were given our weekly pocket money of one shilling (five pence) and were allowed to spend it in the tuck shop set up in the nurses' room.
>
> Visitors were officially allowed every three months. They came by coach which would call at the Crown Hotel, Langdon Hills, before coming on to us.

The sanatorium was almost completely self-sufficient. In the greenhouses near the entrance such things as tomatoes, cucumbers and marrows were grown, while the grounds provided ample supplies of apples, pears, plums and damsons. During the war chickens were kept for meat and eggs. Fresh air was always regarded as the key to recovery from tuberculosis and Mrs. Hickey remembers the bedroom doors and windows being kept wide open regardless of the weather outside. During her sentimental visit

35. Chris Rutter (now Hickey) on the right with her father, sister and a friend in the grounds of the Sanatorium.

36. Nurse Iris Gower who made contact with Mrs. Hickey, a former patient at Langdon Hills Sanatorium, after an interval of over 40 years.

Mrs. Hickey spoke about her favourite nurse at the sanatorium — a young lady called Iris Gower. Thanks to Basildon's *Evening Echo* newspaper, the author managed to trace her to Jeffrey Avenue, Harold Park (Essex) where she was living with her elderly mother. The two were put in touch and in 1988, after 40 years, they met and exchanged memories of their time at Langdon Hills.

Chapter 4

The War Years

The outbreak of war in 1939 resulted in many of the week-end bungalows on Basildon's plotlands being pressed into service as permanent homes for families driven out of London by the bombing. Most people believed that by living in the country they would escape the blitz completely — a false assumption because little Basildon had more than a fair share of incidents considering the rural character of the district. Understandably, however, most of the new settlers felt safer in the wide open spaces of Basildon than in built-up London, and were prepared to put up with poor living conditions to stay there.

By the end of the war in September 1945, the district's official war diary, which recorded every incident to occur in the Basildon, Pitsea, Laindon, Billericay and Wickford area, provided some enlightening statistics. For example, in the six war years 24 people were killed as a result of enemy action, 92 were seriously injured and 454 slightly injured. Property suffered too, 149 homes being completely demolished and 6,100 others being damaged. The records show that the following bombs fell: 941 high explosives; 17,400 incendiaries; 48 oil bombs; 18 flying bombs (V1s); 39 rockets (V2s); 28 parachute mines; 10 anti-personnel bombs and 39 phosphorous bombs. Nine German and 17 British or American planes crashed within Basildon's boundaries, 15 German and seven British fliers being killed.

To many people, this catalogue of incidents was remarkable for such a rural community, but it was because Basildon lay under one of the main routes to London taken by the German bombers. The pilots of many planes used either the River Thames or the Arterial Road to guide them to the capital, and this made south-east Essex very vulnerable to bombs and crashes. The fact also that British fighter stations were situated nearby at Hornchurch and North Weald, and just across the Thames in Kent, made Basildon's skies a principal battlefield during the Battle of Britain.

In addition, the south-east Essex area was dotted with a network of Army anti-aircraft gun emplacements whose object was to intercept the bombers before they could reach London. Many of these guns were supported at night by searchlights which would criss-cross the sky to pick up and try to follow raiders. It was a common and exciting sight to see German planes wriggling and turning in a searchlight's beam in an effort to escape. For those living near these Army bases life was very uncomfortable indeed when raiders sometimes broke ranks and sprayed machine gun bullets down the searchlight beams to try to put them and the guns out of action.

The majority of the bombs which fell in the Basildon district were not aimed at a particular target, unless it was the railway lines or the major roads like the A127 and the A13. Most bombs were dropped indiscriminately by the Germans for self preservation, to lighten their aircraft during moments of danger. The 6,100 properties damaged represented a high proportion of the homes in the area, but many were of sub-standard construction and were knocked over like packs of cards by high explosive bombs, large and small.

The war diary shows that the first bombs to fall on the old Basildon village landed in Gardiner's Lane at 4 p.m. on 30 August 1940. Nine fell, but only six exploded, damaging four cottages and bursting gas and water mains. It was quite remarkable that Gardiner's Lane was also one of the last Basildon roads listed in the diary at the end of the war. The entry concerned a V2 rocket which landed there on 1 March 1945.

When the first air raid siren sounded on the morning of 3 September 1939 to signal the outbreak of war, many people rushed indoors and took cover, expecting an almost immediate air raid. This of course never happened, and it was many months before the majority of British people experienced any direct war action. For the people of Laindon for example, it was exactly a year to the day from the outbreak of war that the first bombs fell on their village. They seriously damaged 11 homes and shops in the High Road near the Arterial Road, and with gas and water mains being hit the road was blocked for several weeks.

Possibly the most jinxed building in Basildon during the war was the Rectory, situated off Rectory Road on a site now partly occupied by the Ford tractor plant. Previously a country house called 'Oliphants', the rectory was severely damaged by two bombs on 17 September 1940, the rector, the Revd. F.W.J. Reynolds, his wife and three children having a lucky escape from injury. Then later in the war on 9 January

37. Some of the air raid wardens and civil defence personnel who did such a valuable service to the community in the Basildon area during the war.

38. Basildon's Rectory (formerly called Oliphants) almost received a direct hit from a bomb in September 1940. The Rector, the late Rev. F.W.J. Reynolds, escaped without injury and is seen with his three children next to the crater.

1945, a V2 rocket struck and rendered the Rectory uninhabitable again. Before repairs could be completed, a second V2 landed almost in the same crater on 11 March 1945, damaging the ill-fated Rectory even more. The Rectory's experience did nothing to allay people's fears about the V2s expressed before — that one strike could well be followed by another from the same launching pad. At Basildon this proved to be the case on more than one occasion.

Like other parts of south Essex, the most memorable day during the Battle of Britain was 5 September 1940, when droves of German planes passed over in broad daylight as the Luftwaffe launched its biggest air attack on London. On that day a British fighter crashed at Markhams Chase, Laindon, its pilot, Pilot Officer Barton from North Weald, escaping uninjured. Another two fighters crashed at Nevendon, one flier, Pilot Officer Webster, plunging to his death when his parachute failed to open. At Gun Hill, Bowers Gifford, a German pilot died in the wreckage of his Messerschmitt 109 which had been shot down.

In the 1940s Basildon was also hit by a number of German land mines, which drifted down on brightly coloured parachutes. Many were of the delayed action variety and several areas had to be evacuated until they were made safe. At Laindon on 21 September 1940, for example, one mine landed in a field north of Dunton Road. Twelve hours later it exploded with a tremendous bang, killing two children who had broken through the security net and gone very close to it. Two other mines landed on the same night in Honeypot Lane, Basildon, and one near the Basildon Road/Church Road junction at Laindon.

Of the 17,000 incendiary bombs to land in Basildon only a few caused serious damage. Most fell in fields and open spaces, burning themselves out harmlessly or becoming buried in the sticky London clay soil. Pitsea and Vange experienced the first incendiary bombardment in the first few months of 1941, but no damage occurred until 19 April, when a bungalow called 'The Oaks' in Timberlog Lane was burned down. In January 1944 one person was killed and three injured when 1,000 incendiaries fell at Paynters Hill, Vange. A week later at Langdon Hills an estimated five thousand fell in the vicinity of the sanatorium in Dry Street.

Basildon's blackest year for damage and casualties was 1944 when everyone in southeast England suffered frightening experiences from the V1 flying bombs, or doodlebugs as they were called. The distinctive throb of the V1s could be heard for miles and as the noise got louder people froze in fear that the engine would cut out. If it did, a deathly silence followed before the pilotless missile hit the ground with a sickening explosion. The doodlebugs did not make deep craters, but the blasts from the explosions caused extensive damage over a wide area of a kind not experienced previously.

One of the first V1 incidents in Basildon killed four cows when the bomb fell on Frierns Farm in Basildon Road on 16 June 1944. The blast damaged the farmhouse and injured one of the occupants. In the following months 17 more flying bombs fell, causing widespread damage to property, including St Nicholas's church, Laindon, which suffered structural damage and broken windows when a V1 fell in Dickens Drive in August. Fifty people were injured and 470 properties damaged — some over two miles away — by another V1 in Northlands Drive, Pitsea, on 7 October 1944. Then at Lee Chapel, Laindon, on 23 October 1944, one person was killed and 100 properties damaged by a V1 and on the same night another was blown up in the air over the same area by a British fighter plane, causing further damage.

As well as the V1s, ordinary high-explosive bombs continued to fall and on 4 February 1944 Basildon suffered one of its worst incidents of the war when five people were killed and 48 injured by a stick of four bombs which devastated the Fairview Road/Southview Road area. About 250 people were made homeless and provided with emergency shelter at Craylands School.

By the end of 1944 the morale of many people was at a low ebb, partly because the war was dragging on and also due to the flying bombs. There was also an uncomfortable feeling that Hitler might still have something up his sleeve which could swing the balance of the whole war. When one of the first V2 rockets fell near White's Farm, Laindon, on 1 December with a tremendous bang, fears increased. In January 1945 another V2 fell at Dickens Drive, Laindon, damaging for a second time many homes which had just been repaired after the doodlebug incident the previous August. Once again St Nicholas's church, Laindon was damaged as well.

For children who grew up in the war years, the battles in the sky, the bombing and the daily hunt for pieces of shrapnel and other souvenirs, caused more excitement than

39. & 40. Wrecked homes in Gordon Road and Fairview Road, Basildon, following a bomb attack in February 1944, which killed five people and left about 250 homeless.

fear. They became accustomed to spending the nights in damp air-raid shelters and having schooling interrupted because of air raids. Numerous school hours were spent huddled in cold brick-built above-ground shelters in school playing fields. They always seemed to have a damp and musty smell about them. It was while being marched to one such shelter at St Nicholas School, Laindon (now Laindon Park School), that the author saw a Messerschmitt 109 fighter crash in flames behind factories on the Arterial Road at Laindon on 5 November 1940. The pilot, Johann Illner, aged 29, baled out, but dislocated a knee and was taken to St Andrew's Hospital, Billericay for treatment.

It was not until almost 49 years later in 1989 that it was disclosed that an interesting metal emblem had been salvaged from the wreckage by a local resident. Painted with the words 'Gott Strafe England' (God strike England), it is a cartoon-style caricature of a bird-like Prime Minister Neville Chamberlain, drawn with a much accentuated long beak, and showing him wearing a bowler hat and carrying a rolled umbrella. The emblem was brought out of hiding and given to the Cater Museum, Billericay, for an

exhibition of wartime memorabilia to mark the 50th anniversary of the outbreak of war. Also in the exhibition was the remains of a German pilot's jacket pulled by another souvenir hunter from the wreckage of a Messerschmitt 110 which crashed at Frithwood, west of Laindon Road, Little Burstead on 2 September 1940.

Eight weeks after that crash the first really serious incident of the war in the Basildon district hit the tiny plotland community of Dunton Hills, where five people were killed by bombs on the same night. The dead were air-raid warden Mrs. Dorothy Mundy, Mrs. Maud Simmons (53), her mother Mrs. Charlotte Gladwin (89) and Helena Penny (16) and Alice Shaw (21). Four of the five were buried in the same grave in Dunton churchyard in a service conducted by the Bishop of Barking, during another air raid. The deaths stunned the small Dunton hamlet and the incident was possibly the worst to hit the district's plotland settlements during the whole war.

An outstanding memory for hundreds in south-east Essex during the war was seeing the massive build-up of troops and equipment along the roads prior to the invasion of France on D-Day in June

41. Mr. Ted Wright, Curator of the Cater Museum, Billericay, with the Chamberlain emblem retrieved from the wreckage of a crashed German Messerschmitt 109 at Laindon in November 1940.

42. & 43.   Homes wrecked by seven bombs which fell on the Dunton Hills estate on 8 November 1940. Five people were killed.

44. Nevendon's Dad's Army — members of the local Home Guard pictured with their dog mascot in the 1940s.

1944. The hush-hush build-up saw main roads like the Arterial Road numbered with parking places for thousands of Army vehicles and items of equipment. They appeared overnight and disappeared equally silently just before D-Day. For days the open air of Noak Hill Road between Laindon and Billericay became home for thousands of troops forced to camp out on the roadside before moving one stage further forward towards Tilbury Docks or the Kent ports. Looking back it was remarkable that only a few years earlier Basildon had been, like many other places in southern England, preparing for a German invasion of our country.

Most people have their own particular memories of the war years in Basildon. For ex-Langdon Hills resident Eric Grant, his was the day when baked apples could be seen hanging from trees in Langdon Hills after a German Dornier plane had crashed in flames on 15 September 1940. He remembers standing with his parents outside their home as the German plane was strafed with bullets by a British fighter. 'It changed direction several times' he said.

> It was obviously in great trouble with its engines knocked out and at one time it was drifting straight towards us. The fighter then hit it again and it turned a complete right angle, missed us and plunged into a garden in Gladstone Road. It was so low in the end that it actually went underneath the telegraph wires before coming to a halt and bursting into flames.

Those first on the scene found three of the crew dead in the trees, but by the time Eric was allowed to go, all that remained was the wreckage . . . and the baked apples!

45. Laindon Home Guard outside their headquarters, rather appropriately called the *Fortune of War* public house.

46. Laindon Home Guard in full battle gear and armed, during a break from a training manoeuvre.

Another Langdon Hills man, Mr. L.W. Green, now living in New Zealand, remembers emerging from an Anderson shelter with his mother in Roseberry Avenue and finding a huge crater in the road outside their home. The last of a stick of four, the bomb caused a great deal of damage, but the Greens' home escaped without even a broken window. Another of Mr. Green's wartime memories was the discovery of unexploded incendiary bombs which fell on a timber wharf at Vange. On examination the bombs were found to contain sawdust instead of magnesium — a case of sabotage by German workers? We will never know.

Other people remember the war for a variety of reasons, some very small but personal. Mrs. Grace Wolfenden, later of Butneys, Basildon, had fond memories of dancing lessons for sixpence a time at the Hut Club in Samuel Road, Langdon Hills. For their money the girls and boys would also get a cup of cocoa and a sticky bun, except when funds were low when they would be asked to share one bun between two. She also recalls travelling each day to London on the 5.50 a.m. train to work in a canteen at the London Docks.

> We never knew what we were going to find in the mornings after the air raids. One night I walked to the top of Crown Hill at Langdon Hills and could see London ablaze in the distance. I cried my eyes out because I thought there would be nothing left the following day.

By the end of the war the miles of unmade roads in Basildon district and the hundreds of tiny properties had become a major problem for Billericay Urban District Council. With servicemen returning from the war and preferring to live in the countryside rather than return to bomb-hit London, the population soon hit the 20,000 mark — a three-fold increase on pre-war figures. With so many of these people living in poor, unhealthy conditions in properties which sometimes had a rateable value of £10 or less, the council had a problem which could be ignored no longer. To carry out all the necessary work itself, including the making up of 78 miles of rough roads, was an undertaking which was impossible to finance out of the low income from rates. If it was forced to foot the bill, the council knew that the rates would have to increase dramatically, forcing people to move elsewhere. In London, at the same time, the lack of new housing to replace the thousands of homes destroyed by the bombing, together with a greater demand for better housing by the returning servicemen, created a huge problem for the London boroughs. It was little wonder that those with properties in the plotlands of south Essex decided to go and live in them permanently. This increased the likelihood of a serious health problem developing because whole areas of the plotlands were without sewers or mains water. With many of the properties only being of wooden construction, there was also a serious fire hazard from the use of paraffin for heating and lighting. If a fire did occur, the impassable nature of many of the roads in the winter months made access by the rescue and fire services very difficult indeed.

The influx of people to the area also put a great strain on local services such as schools and hospitals at a time when councils had insufficient funds even to make up for years of wartime neglect. It was understandable, therefore, that Billericay Council considered it had an outstanding case for government help.

Some of the happiest people of all were those who actually lived on the plotlands. The majority were perfectly content enjoying their way of life in the countryside and for that privilege were prepared to put up with 'little inconveniences' like unmade roads and lack of services. But Billericay Council wanted action, and the chance soon came . . . with government backing as a bonus.

Chapter 5

The Creation of the New Town

It was almost by accident that Basildon became a serious contender to be one of the seven New Towns to be built around London after the war. Such New Towns were first suggested in Sir Patrick Abercrombie's 1944 Greater London Area Plan. Under this plan, new towns were proposed within countryside green belts to counteract the unbalanced growth all round London which was typical of the inter-war period. They would be properly designed self-contained communities in which industry would provide employment for most inhabitants, who would be spared time and energy wasted in long daily journeys to work.

This concept was not new. The idea had been originated by Mr. Ebenezer Howard who, without either wealth or influential connections, lived to see the birth of his idea in the so-called Garden Cities of Letchworth and Welwyn in Hertfordshire. Even under the Abercrombie plan Essex was written in as a possible site for two of the New Towns, the early suggestions being Harlow, Ongar and Margaretting.

When the war ended, the country's new socialist government led by Clement Attlee accepted the recommendations of the Greater London Plan in principle and then went a step further by passing the New Towns Act of 1946. As a non-controversial measure the Government then designated the first five New Towns in the Home Counties and started investigations into possible sites for the other two. It was when two of these sites, at Margaretting and Ongar, were rejected that Billericay Urban District Council stepped in and with support from Essex County Council made a bid for a New Town in its area.

The force behind the suggestion was Billericay's ambitious Council Clerk, Mr. Alma Hatt, who long before had seen such a town as the only solution to his council's serious problems of planning chaos, unmade roads and a worsening housing shortage. In a New Town Mr. Hatt also saw the prospects for more employment opportunities for the council's electorate and a vast improvement in the district's prosperity through the injection of government funds for the provision of services and amenities. He knew, too, that the creation of a new town would lead to a substantial rise in the council's income from the rates.

He had to put together a strong enough case not only to get the support of the government and the county council, but also to persuade the majority of his own district councillors that the New Town was a dream solution to the district's problems. This latter task was not as easy as it sounded because some councillors were still very parochial in outlook and unwilling to upset their electorate. For many voters the idea of a New Town in their midst was like a red rag to a bull and they were vehemently opposed to it. Mr. Hatt, however, was a shrewd man and he adopted the tactic of persuading a few influential councillors in the first instance in the expectation that they would sway the others in favour of the idea. His case revolved around the fact that almost without spending a penny, Billericay Council would see its population and

47. An aerial view of the old village of Basildon in March 1954 before the New Town centre was started. One third of the way down the picture can be seen the Fenchurch Street to Southend railway line and the railway bridge at the junction of Clay Hill Road.

consequently its revenue from the rates increase substantially, with the government footing most of the bill for the new development. One of the main points he stressed to those councillors who were local businessmen was that every person brought into Basildon by the development was a potential customer for them.

By this approach, Hatt gradually enlisted enough support and on 26 October 1946 he put the council's case for the New Town in Basildon in an official letter to the Minister of Town and Country Planning. The case was strengthened by the support of the East End boroughs of East and West Ham which were both interested in south-east Essex as a possible provider of housing sites for their homeless and those living in poor conditions. They particularly liked the Basildon area because of the strong ties which already existed with it since many residents there had come from East London originally. Another factor was that Essex County Council had been concerned for some years about the state of the Laindon and Pitsea area and the large scattered comunity which had grown up there. Put together, it all added up to a strong case for a New Town at Basildon and on 25 May 1948 the government announced provisional approval of it.

By the time of the official announcement, rumours of the proposal had been circulating around the district fanned by the newspapers for many months. During that time the opposition grew from a whimper at the start to a very loud bark, the most vociferous opponents being the owners of freehold land and property who suddenly realised that their life's work was threatened. The first organised opposition came with the setting up of Laindon Residents Protection Association in 1948. The association's main concern was the loss of freehold rights and a battle cry 'A freehold for a freehold' was introduced to very good effect. This soon spread not only to other residents' groups formed in Basildon, Pitsea and Vange, but to other parts of the country where home and land owners were being threatened in a similar way.

By the time the Minister of Town and Country Planning, the Rt. Hon. Lewis Silkin, bravely came into the lion's den at Laindon on 7 October 1948 to explain his proposals, feelings were running very high and several thousand people turned up at Laindon School to confront him. Mr. Silkin received a stormy reception, but in spite of numerous interruptions he managed to leave few people in any doubt that a miracle would be needed if the New Towns plans were to be halted and reversed. In his speech Mr. Silkin said it was not his intention to inflict injury or harm on anyone as a result of the New Town proposals. But he pointed out that the government had a duty and a wider responsibility to help others like people in East and West Ham where German bombs had destroyed one in four homes, leaving 20,000 people desperate for accommodation.

By the following January (1949) the designation of Basildon New Town was confirmed and the first Development Corporation board was appointed to start the redevelopment task. The chairman, Sir Lancelot Keay, was a past President of the R.I.B.A. and a Director of Housing for Liverpool. In the following months the government approved the appointment of other corporation board members including Mr. E.L. Protheroe (deputy chairman), Mr. M. Auliff, Mr. N. Davenport, Mrs. E.J. Gregory (former mayor of West Ham), Mr. F.C. Jobson (a local J.P.), Mrs. W.M. Knight, Mrs. D.M. Sargent and Col. S.A. Smith, M.C. In May 1949 Brigadier W.G.D. Knapton took over as the Corporation's first General Manager, and his team included Mr. Charles Boniface as solicitor, the start for him of an association with the corporation which spanned 26 years, including 21 years as general manager.

The official designation document stated that the New Town was for the twofold purpose of taking overspill population and industry from the London area and for upgrading and eradicating the areas of inferior quality development. Billericay council was therefore relieved of the major burden of improving the area they administered south of the A127 road, but it still had to tackle a smaller similar problem in the towns of Billericay and Wickford where some of the road conditions were just as bad as in Basildon.

The designation document also stated that the government through its agent, Basildon Development Corporation, would bear the major development costs including the purchase of land and buildings, construction of roads, drainage, houses, shops and small industrial units. Local authorities such as Essex County Council and Billericay U.D.C. would provide back-up services such as schools, libraries and clinics as the town expanded. By agreement, other public and private facilities, such as hospitals and the supply of various services, would be introduced 'as needed', or at least that was the plan at the time. It did not always prove to be the case.

The task faced by Basildon Development Corporation was possibly the most difficult of all the corporations set up in the Home Counties at that time. For one thing the designated area of 7,818 acres was an awkward shape to plan, being six miles long and three miles wide. It was made more difficult by the fact that it was bisected by a railway line and bordered by hills to the south and poorly drained land to the north. Some 4,500 acres of the area consisted of wilderness, scrubland and thousands of plots containing 5,600 sub-standard properties. The land and buildings in the designated area were in 30,000 different ownerships, a large proportion of them being unknown, a fact which gave the corporation a huge headache in years to come.

Another problem which had to be overcome was to produce a Master Plan of development for Basildon which would accommodate an existing population of 25,000 and integrate them with the newcomers to make a socially and economically better urban community. It was for this latter reason that the corporation successfully argued almost from the start that the original 50,000 target population figure set for the town was insufficient. They believed 80,000 to be a more realistic figure if the two existing communities of Laindon and Pitsea — $3\frac{1}{2}$ miles apart — were to be joined together for the unity of the town.

The change in the population target was one of the major points put forward by the corporation at a public inquiry into the first master plan held on 13 June 1951. An indication of the government's intention to press ahead at full speed was confirmed by the fact that the plan received approval within nine weeks.

The chief elements of the plan included a suggested road pattern; the location of the town centre approximately in the centre of the designated area; the location of industry mainly on the northern side near the A127 Arterial Road; and the creation of 15 housing neighbourhoods of different sizes. The plan catered for an estimated 20,000 people to be employed in consumer industries and services and for about 16,000 to work on the industrial estates, which would be no more than 10-15 minutes away by cycle or bus from most homes. In his letter of approval, the government minister suggested that the corporation's estimate of an eventual 16,000 workers on the industrial estates could be too high. Time has since proved that far from being an over-estimate the figure turned out to be about half of the number employed on the estates by the time the corporation was wound up in 1986.

The original master plan was based on the fundamental principle that the town would be a self-supporting self-contained community, although it was always expected that seven thousand or so of the original 25,000 inhabitants would continue to travel out of the area to work. Although over the years numerous changes of detail were made, the master plan stood the test of time well for almost 40 years in spite of national and economic influences which affected housing, industry, commercial development and employment.

Possibly the biggest changes were made to cope with the growth of car ownership over the years. When the first plan was drawn up few people owned cars and only limited provision was made for garages and parking spaces. The estate roads were also very narrow, although this was partly due to financial restrictions placed on development by the government. In later years as access for both residents and emergency vehicles became a problem because of parked cars on the estates, both the development corporation and the district council were forced to spend many thousands of pounds providing additional off-street parking on the old estates.

Car ownership also had a marked effect on the planning of new shopping areas, including Laindon and Pitsea. Much more space was required for cars than originally anticipated and this caused quite a problem in the town centre, where outward expansion was virtually impossible due to the adjacent housing estates built before the town's target population increased to over one hundred and thirty thousand.

By 1960 the government officially recognised that the population of Basildon was likely to exceed 80,000 even without natural growth, and a new target of 106,000 was set. Hardly was the ink dry on the approval of the revised plan when the corporation was ordered to investigate if a population of 140,000 could be accommodated without changing the size of the designated area. A public inquiry was held in February 1967 and a new master plan was eventually approved for a population of 133,600. The reduction from 140,000 was mainly due to the tough fight put up by Essex County Council, local environmentalists and residents' groups in opposing the creation of new housing areas in and around the country parks and beauty spots of Langdon Hills in the south-west corner of the town. Their opposition led to two housing neighbourhoods being deleted from the plan by the minister, thus reducing the population by some 6,600 people. But this was not all. Later a third housing estate was dropped following local opposition before the detailed proposals were submitted for government approval, and then a fourth housing area was taken out by the minister himself. This was really the icing on the cake for the environmentalists who fought hard for many years to protect the country parks, the woodlands and the wildlife in the Langdon Hills beauty spots.

After that the Development Corporation went quietly out of existence in 1986 leaving the local protesters savouring a victory which can only benefit the quality of life for thousands in the future. This became even more certain in 1989 when it was announced by the corporation's successor, the Commission for New Towns, that the Essex Naturalist Trust was to take over the management of nearly 500 acres of open countryside at Langdon Hills as a nature reserve. The purchase of the land from the Commission by the Trust was made possible because of a multi-thousand pound legacy from surveyor and conservationist Mr. Herbert Langdon Dowsett.

This was a dream ending for people like Langdon Hills campaigner Stanley Hollands of Bruce Grove whose long battle to protect the open spaces drew praise from the Minister of Environment in his public inquiry decision statement in 1967. Said Mr. Hollands: 'When we started out we never thought we stood much chance against the might of the development corporation but we have won a conclusive victory and I am delighted'.

Chapter 6

The New Town Pioneers

A very special day in the history of Basildon was 18 June 1951, the date when the very first new tenants moved into the first few houses to be completed in the New Town. For most newcomers, a brand new house with 'a proper kitchen' and a garden was a dream come true after the horrendous living conditions they had experienced previously in London's East End. For the Development Corporation, too, the arrival of the first tenants was a special occasion and the culmination of months of planning since the board had been appointed in 1949. The first housing contract to be signed by the Corporation in September 1950 was for 39 houses to be built by C.S. Wiggins at Vange.

Betty and John Walker were actually the first couple to get the keys of a new house, then 61 Redgrave Road. They were quickly followed on the same day by Eric and Marjorie Hawkridge and their three children at No. 63 and then Stan and Phyllis Martin at No. 59. The Martins previously lived in a Nissen hut provided as temporary housing at Custom House in East London. They hated every minute of it and longed for a home where they could settle down and bring up their family 'in a nice clean environment'. Basildon gave them, like hundreds of other young families, that opportunity. A skilled carpenter, Stan Martin was earning a good wage on ships in London's dockland, but when he heard about the need for building workers in Basildon, and that houses were being offered to those who volunteered, he and Phyllis had no hesitation in applying. By June 1951 the Martins' possessions were all packed and they headed east for a new life in Basildon. Phyllis said:

> I can remember it like yesterday. Redgrave Road was in the middle of countryside and the house allocated to us was one of the first six to be finished. They were lovely and contained a living room, three bedrooms, a kitchen, a bathroom and a nice garden. It was like moving into paradise.

48. Mrs. Betty Walker. She and her husband John were the first tenants to move into a New Town house, on 18 June 1951.

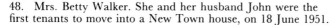

53

The Martins' three children, Jimmy, Ronnie and Christine, also have happy recollections of their childhood in Basildon. Christine, who still lives in the town with her husband and two children, recalled:

> What was so good was that we were surrounded by countryside and there was an orchard at the back of our house. In Vange Hill Drive nearby there was a bungalow where they kept cows, horses and chickens. It was smashing for us children although Dad was not so happy when the cows one day ate his cabbages.

Christine also remembers that there was an amazing variety of wildlife around the estate, including badgers, foxes and squirrels which came right up to their back door.

When her children were older and going their own way, Phyllis returned to work as a telephonist first with Basildon telephone exchange, and later with factories such as Yardley, Marconi and Ford. She ended up by joining Basildon Council.

Eric and Marjorie Hawkridge have never forgotten the celebration which centred around the day they became Basildon's second tenants. There to greet them was the Development Corporation's first general manager, Brigadier Knapton, and Lady Whitmore, wife of the then Lord Lieutenant of Essex, who gave his name to Whitmore Way, the first main feeder road to be built. The Hawkridges, with children Eric, aged five, and Robert, aged 11, came from Eric's parents' home in West Ham where they had shared a two-up, two-down property. They had been on the council waiting list for four years and had little hope of getting a home of their own.

In Basildon they were delighted with their new house. Mr. Hawkridge remembered:

> We could not believe our luck. One of the things we most appreciated was hot running water in the bathroom, bringing to an end the days in East London where we had to boil up water in kettles to have a bath. After the slums of London a home in the country was out of this world and we took to the life like fish to water in spite of the fact that we had a job finding £1 12s. 4d. a week for the rent.

A foreman bricklayer with a firm called Jenners, Mr. Hawkridge travelled to work from Ilford in the back of a lorry before being allocated his house. 'When I first saw the place it was just a village with a little post office.' Marjorie has fond memories of walking with other young mothers with their babies from Vange to the shops in Pitsea. If the weather was bad they would catch a Campbell's bus from Bull Road for a penny fare.

The Hawkridges' taste for adventure led them to leave the New Town in 1956 to seek a new life in Australia, but Marjorie was homesick and by 1960 they were back in England to live on Canvey Island.

Another of the pioneering first families at Vange were the Smiths — Albert, Rose and baby Carol. They had lived in one room in East Ham since Albert had returned from being a prisoner of war in 1945. With the arrival of baby Carol the one room seemed to get smaller every day and, desperate for a home of his own, Albert wrote a letter of complaint to the then Housing Minister, Aneurin Bevan, the pioneer of the National Health Service. Albert said, 'I told him that England was not the land fit for heroes the Government had promised and that heroes should at least have somewhere decent to live'. The Minister referred the letter to East Ham Council who quickly wrote to tell him he could get a house in Basildon if he was prepared to work there as a bricklayer. Albert took little persuading and on Guy Fawkes night 1951 he and his wife moved into Redgrave Road. Like many other men Albert found the work very tough. The hours were long and the conditions on the building sites were atrocious with sticky

clay often knee high. He stuck it out because he needed the money — 2s. 6d. an hour —
to pay the rent and to help raise his family. Albert sadly lost his wife in 1987, and
when Basildon's 40th anniversary was celebrated two years later, he was still living in
the same house he had moved into 37 years previously.

49. The Barstable area in 1948, before the New Town. The railway bridge (left) and the Timberlog Land junction
with Bull Road (now Timberlog Lane and Clay Hill Road) can be clearly seen, together with the Gordon Road
and Fairview Road estate — the two straight white roads on the left hand side.

The early tenants in Vange were quickly followed by newcomers in the two other
new housing areas of Fryerns and Barstable. The conditions were somewhat difficult at
first, their homes being situated on building sites which were a sea of mud in the winter.
The nearest shops were at Vange or Pitsea, although other small shops did exist in
Timberlog Lane and in Bull Road.

As the estates grew, mobile traders proliferated until it was possible to buy green-
grocery, groceries, bread and even fish and chips from a whole host of enterprising

tradesmen who toured the estates at all hours in old converted vans. The first shops to
be built on a new estate were in Pendle Drive, Fryerns. They belonged to the Co-op
and were opened in August 1952. The grocery shop was managed by a man who went
on to achieve an outstandingly long record of public service to the town, Councillor
Alfred Dove.

When Alf became the first Basildon New Town tenant to be elected chairman of
Basildon Council in 1963, after being a councillor since 1956, the *Basildon Standard*
newspaper wrote:

> From errand boy to shop manager, from tenants' treasurer to Council chairman . . . that's Alf Dove's
> route to fame. He likes natty hats, eating well, people in general, gardening, modern art and
> Basildon. He does not own a car — 'can't afford one' — would like to spend more time with his
> children, to try his hand at oil painting and to see everyone who needs a house getting one.

Born in Shoreditch, Alf first discovered Basildon after being offered the job as manager
of the new Co-op shop. He cycled down from Dagenham expecting to find a huge
expanse of town, but was amazed by what he saw. 'When I got to Basildon I asked
someone the way to the New Town and was told, "This is it".' By sheer coincidence,
the first person Mr. Dove met was Mrs. Gladys Taylor who, like him, later became a
district councillor and also a prominent worker for the local community association,
particularly in the campaign to get a hospital for the town. Once he had moved into
his shop and then to a new house in The Fryth which was still his home in 1989, Alf
took to Basildon straight away. It gave him his first roots since boyhood and from the
first day he was sure the town would be his home for the rest of his life.

Of the first years, Alf said that the pioneers had to find their own amusement and to
look around for places in the vicinity for an afternoon out. Lake Meadows at Billericay,
which was a 30-minute bus ride away, was one favourite place. 'Few people had cars
mainly because the majority of tenants had a struggle to pay their rents and bring up
their children. A car was a real luxury.' Despite the odd grumble Alf would still live
nowhere else. 'New towns were different. They had better standards of housing for
ordinary working class people. They were homes with central heating and bathrooms.
For most it was heaven.'

On becoming the first New Town chairman of the Urban District Council in 1963,
Alf hit newspaper headlines all over the country and as far away as Australia because
he used to arrive for civic functions on his motor scooter with his chain of office dangling
round his neck. Before his year of office ended the Council had bought a civic car and
he used it for the first time on 15 February 1964 to go to the opening of the ambulance
station in Basildon town centre. Since then Alf has attended hundreds of functions and
meetings in the town and in 1990 was still a hardworking member of the council for
the Fryerns Ward in which he still lives.

Like so many things in the early days, new firsts were being chalked up almost every
week, like the first letter box in Whitmore Way, the first telephone box and the first
public house (*The Crane*), in Pendle Drive. At the same time the housing estates were
mushrooming westwards across the fields and farmland of old Basildon, and the new
Cranes Industrial Estate was growing alongside the A127 Arterial Road. By 1951 the
network of roads on the estate had been completed and the first factory, for the South-
East Essex Wholesale Dairies, was in business. The majority of the early settlers were
building workers, but as the industrial estate expanded a greater proportion looked to

50. The first New Towner to become Chairman of Basildon Urban District Council, Councillor Alf Dove, with his motor scooter on which he travelled to official functions before he was given a civic car.

51. Chairman Alf Dove proudly wearing the chain of office during his year as Council Chairman in 1963/4. Also in the picture (left to right) are Mrs. J. Kefford (Girl Guide Commissioner), Mrs. E.J. Gregory (former Mayor of West Ham), Mrs. Dove, Rev. William Winfield (Rural Dean) and Mr. Fred Pittock (Scout Commissioner).

factory work for their livelihood. The biggest grumbles were the seemingly high rents of the New Town houses when compared with the old council properties in London, plus the country-rate pay levels in the factories.

Coming from cramped accommodation in London most newcomers brought little furniture with them and only in rare cases was it adequate to fill a three-bedroom house. Most homes were sparsely furnished and only very few had the luxury of fitted carpets, the majority making do with mats and thin floor coverings bought from Pitsea market or mobile traders. Hire purchase provided a way out for many families, but it often led them into debt and becoming more and more frustrated with the low wages. The men were forced to work long hours of overtime to boost their pay packets and often had little time or energy to spend with their families. It was little wonder that some marriages fell apart and couples split up and headed back to London to be near their relatives.

Possibly the biggest problem facing the early settlers — particularly young mothers — was loneliness, caused by the fact that they had been deposited in new homes in a strange place away from friends and relatives. They also had to spend long hours alone while husbands were at work. So many young mothers complained of being lonely and homesick that a problem of epidemic proportions, which the media called 'The New Town Blues', made national headline news. The town's first tenants' association at Fryerns even called in a psychiatrist to propose solutions to it. He explained that although young families had left behind stressful, bad housing conditions in London and now had 'nice homes in the country in Basildon', it was not the complete solution for happiness. Living on a new estate in what was still a rural area was in stark contrast to East Ham High Street with the convenience of shops and entertainment on the doorstep and relatives and friends nearby. Even a visit to the fish-and-chip shop was a social occasion in London, a place to chat with neighbours while waiting to be served. Such social contacts were missed in Basildon.

The New Town Blues highlighted Basildon's greatest need in those early days — social facilities. But it took some time before the Development Corporation dug deep to find £3,600 for three small wooden community huts on the first three estates. At Fryerns a labour force recruited by the tenants' association volunteered to build the hall on condition that the money saved would be spent on making it larger or on additional equipment. There was hope that the tenants in Vange and Barstable would also build their halls, but they were never so well organised as at Fryerns, and in both cases the Corporation had to call in builders to finish the job.

The Fryerns hall at the rear of houses at the junction of The Fryth and Southcote Crescent was finished first, entirely by a team of forty or so volunteers who worked evenings and weekends to see the job through. It became a valuable social facility and meeting place in that part of the town until for many purposes it was superseded by the much larger Fryerns Community Centre built in Whitmore Way in 1960.

Much of the credit for pressurising the authorities into doing something about the lack of social provision and other facilities was due to the work of the tenants' associations on the three new estates. The first was formed at Fryerns in June 1952 as a result of a road accident when little Douglas Findlay, aged three, was knocked down by a lorry when going to meet his father. Luckily for Douglas, ambulance officer Bill Jones was passing the scene at the time and he helped save the boy's life by getting him to

Billericay Hospital quickly. The accident highlighted one of the many problems facing the new tenants: the condition of the old roads, which were having to take far heavier traffic than ever before. At the time of the accident only 50 families lived in the Cranes area of Fryerns, but there were sufficient among them to provide the nucleus of the tenants'group formed two days later at a Sunday morning meeting.

Called F.A.T.A. (Fryerns Area Tenants Association), its first Secretary was Mr. William (Bill) Ferrier, who later became its Chairman and President. He was also behind much of the activity to get the Basildon tenants a better service from the corporation and the local council, in spite of the fact that on arriving in Basildon from West Ham he had vowed to take a rest from his previous public work which revolved around the Labour Party and the trade union movement. Together with Alf Dove, who became the treasurer of F.A.T.A., another leading member was the secretary Ted Parsons who lived in Pendle Drive. Ted and his wife Louisa had lived in a Nissen hut in East Ham, like some other new Basildonians, before coming to the new town with their two young sons. By day Ted was a carpenter on the building sites, while his evenings were spent largely on tenants' association business.

The first years of Basildon provided the churches with a great opportunity to play a leading role in the community for the benefit of the town and its people. Some denominations took a long time to realise the potential for growth, or to give help where it was needed most, to the homesick or lonely in the new dwellings. Instead, the activities of the churches were mainly confined to the old villages of Laindon, Pitsea and Vange and they were generally out of reach and out of touch with the newcomers lost in the wilderness of the new estates.

One young man who saw the challenge and grasped it was the Methodist minister, Rev. Donald Shaw, who will never forget his one year in Basildon in 1953 when he wore out several pairs of shoes and almost as many bicycle tyres. He arrived in Basildon for his first appointment straight from Cambridge University. Officially he was a probationary minister for the Leigh-on-Sea circuit with pastoral oversight for the Methodist Society in Pitsea, but when he was appointed he was asked to pioneer Methodism in Basildon as one of his main tasks. Mr. Shaw's first impression of the new town area was that 'it was rather drab and a place on which someone had rained hundreds of tiny bungalows. They were dotted about everywhere. Little did I realise that I would find myself living in one with no w.c., just an elsan at the bottom of the garden'.

Under his leadership the first Methodist services of worship in the new town were held at the home of Mr. Newman-Brown, an architect with Basildon Corporation, and his wife. Services held in the lounge were initially attended by seven or eight people, but numbers increased as the weeks went by. Eventually larger premises became essential and these were found by converting an old empty bungalow in Nelson Road, called Hillview, which stood in the middle of a waterlogged field. In 1988 Mr. Shaw wrote:

> The Methodist Society provided money to buy 50 chairs and a few tables and work was started to transform the bungalow into a place both for worship and meetings.
>
> We decided in the first instance to form a Girls' Life Brigade company and a women's meeting, for which we had leadership, but I shall never forget the week-end work started at Hillview. The rain never stopped for days and our biggest problem was getting to the bungalow from the road.

52. The Methodists began to worship in Basildon in 1953, in this wooden bungalow in Nelson Road.

Mr. Newman-Brown and I got soaked laying paving stones so that people would not get too muddy. It was still raining on the Monday afternoon for the first women's meeting and also for the G.L.B. meeting in the evening.

What a start, but there was a spirit of real adventure about it all and this is what remains with me most strongly even now. It was real pioneering work carried out by a few loyal and determined methodists.

An important feature of Mr. Shaw's work consisted of just being seen around the estates either walking or on his bicycle. One thing which surprised him was the number of new mothers who would stop him and ask them to church them in their homes. Most of them were Anglicans who still retained what is now an old fashioned idea that mothers do not take out their babies until they had been churched. 'I did this gladly for them even though most had no connection at all with Methodism', he said.

Another memory of those early days was how quickly some roads developed a certain character, with some houses being kept beautifully with gardens a joy to see. In other parts neglect of house and garden quickly became very apparent. Of course in the first years of the new town nobody was allowed to buy a house built by the development corporation and all the occupants were tenants regardless of their income or social status.

Greatly due to Rev. Shaw's work, Methodism expanded in the town before a decision to abandon the bungalow church and to move to the premises of Gordon Hall free church in Timberlog Lane was in part responsible for ending his happy association with the town. It was quite obvious even in those days that Basildon would eventually be large enough to become a Circuit in its own right, but being only a probationer Rev. Shaw was ineligible to become its first Superintendent. Writing later he said that he was against the merger with Gordon Hall because he considered the Methodists would be submerging their image into a free church which had very limited appeal, like so many others in Essex. 'I also felt it quashed the spirit of adventure and newness which was beginning to become part of the life of the small Methodist community we had created in Basildon'.

Inevitably the Basildon Methodist Circuit did materialise and one of its early superintendents was a dynamic man, the Rev. Ronald Gibbins, who after seven years in Basildon went on to become Minister of Wesley's Chapel in London — the mother church of the world's 51-million Methodist community. Mr. Gibbins looked back on his time in Basildon from 1957 to 1964 as an enjoyable experience. 'There was never a dull moment', he recalled.

Not a person to sit back and wait for things to happen, he caused a stir in 1960 when he sought election to Basildon council as an independent candidate in a strong Labour ward. It was the first time a minister had stood for council and his decision so upset the local socialists that they turned out all their big guns and party workers on polling day in an effort to beat him. He lost by only 375 votes, and relegated the Tory candidate to third place in the poll. Rev. Gibbins soon shook off the defeat and then launched into a campaign opposing the granting of drinks licences to a number of new establishments in Basildon including the Locarno ballroom. He got his views through to the public by producing and circulating his own four-page newspaper throughout the town. The minister was never out of the headlines for long, and there was one occasion when he invited the Beatles, who were then in their heyday, to open his youth club in Basildon. The pop group did not come, but because of the publicity hundreds of youngsters turned up to join. On leaving Basildon the Rev. Gibbins became Superintendent of the East End Mission for 14 years while his wife started a university career, training teachers in religious education.

Another leading churchman in Basildon's first years was a Baptist minister, the Rev. Charles B. Phillimore. He arrived in 1953 after giving up a prosperous career as a surgical and dental instrument technician in London's West End. The son of a lay preacher with over 50 years' experience, Rev. Phillimore described himself as 'an old-fashioned preacher' in his first newspaper interview on arrival in the new town. Like the Methodists he also started his operations in a tiny bungalow off Timberlog Lane which eventually became due for demolition. He stayed in Basildon for 14 years during which time he masterminded the building of the New Town's first purpose-built church in Whitmore Way, opened in 1954, and the establishment of a thriving Baptist community in the town.

As Basildon grew, the other churches followed the example set by the Methodists and Baptists and began to take much more interest in the new settlers. The old 13th-century Holy Cross church in Church Road became the centre of Church of England operations under the rector of Laindon-cum-Basildon, Rev. William Winfield, until the first new Church of England building, St Andrew's church in The Fremnells, was opened in Fryerns in 1955 under the priest-in-charge, Rev. John King.

53. Holy Cross church in Church Road, when it was the centre of Church of England activities in Basildon.

54. Basildon's second Rural Dean, Rev. Arthur Dunlop (second from the right), at an ordination service at St Martin's church. On the left is Rev. E.C. Telford who was then Rector of Langdon Hills.

Most of the Roman Catholics worshipped at Vange and Langdon Hills until their first church, St Basil's, was built in Luncies Road. The first service there was held in October 1956.

Later, various other new churches were built, including the £40,000 church of St Martin-le-Tours in the town centre which became the flagship for Anglican operations in the town after its consecration in 1962. The first Rural Dean at St Martin's and the first to occupy the new rectory next door was the Rev. Winfield, who had been living temporarily in the development corporation house in Priors Close while his new home was being built. Previously Mr. Winfield and his family had lived in the nine-room Basildon rectory which was sacrificed to make way for Ford's tractor plant. In 1965 he was succeeded by the Rev. Arthur Dunlop who thus returned to the parish where he had been brought up. In those days he was head server at St Nicholas's church, Laindon, and a leader of the Boy Scout troop connected to the church. Rev. Dunlop remained Rural Dean until 1972, when he handed over to Rev. P. Grimwood.

Undoubtedly Basildon's most go-ahead Rural Dean has been the Rev. (now Canon) Lionel Webber, who after his arrival in 1976 put St Martin's on the map as a leading feature of the community.

In addition to raising the money to move a church organ originally at St Erkenwald's, Southend, and getting it installed in St Martin's, Mr. Webber also opened his church for various activities including exhibitions. One very controversial exhibition, which attracted 17,000 people in 1983, was about the Auschwitz atrocities. Later he launched a scheme to provide St Martin's with stained glass windows and in 1988 the first of these was put in.

Most of Basildon's new residents had little experience of organising people into social or voluntary groups. But when the need was there, many tackled the job with enthusiasm and made very good work of it. One such man was Charlie West who 'accidentally' became involved in running a boys' football team and ended up organising one of the most successful boys' clubs for miles around. Charlie was aged 35 when he came to Basildon with his wife Jessie in 1953. They had been on West Ham's housing waiting list for six years and decided to give Basildon a try because it was their only hope of getting a home of their own.

A soccer lover, Charlie had not been in the town very long when he found himself organising an impromptu soccer match for children on the Cranes estate. He and the boys enjoyed it so much that he decided to form a team to play regular matches. For some years the tiny community hut off Southcote Crescent was used as a meeting place until, after a great deal of hard work raising money, the club built its own headquarters in Cranes Farm Road in 1965. Over the years Fryerns Boys' Club won countless trophies and individual honours in all age groups all over Essex. They also provided boys for national and county representative teams and saw a number of their players go on to play professional football with clubs such as West Ham, Southend United and Charlton. Unfortunately Fryern Boys' Club folded when the clubhouse was burned down mysteriously in the 1980s and Charlie, who became an honorary life member of the club, is now happy just to sit back and reflect on all the happy memories which his boys brought to him and the town in the club's long and successful history.

Two other men who also worked tirelessly to put Basildon on the youth soccer map were Bill Parfitt and Bill Cove, who achieved fantastic success while organising Basildon

Minors football club. This was the club which provided the first New Town boy to turn professional — Ray Smith, who joined Southend United in August 1962.

Another typical pioneer who chalked up a very creditable record of success in helping to make Basildon a better place was Mrs. Eve Baylis. An early arrival in 1954, Eve and her husband had not been in Basildon long when she was invited to attend a tenants' meeting on the Fryerns estate. She was so impressed by the work being done by the committee to help the newcomers like herself that she volunteered to help and before the evening was out was elected the association's secretary. In addition to her work for the tenants' association and also as secretary for the Association of Tenants from all the New Towns, Eve was a founder member of Basildon's Red Cross branch and also helped to run the Basildon Citizens' Advice Bureau from 1957 until 1974. Over the years she served on a total of 33 local committees and at the age of 75 was still involved with voluntary work as a tenants' representative. Her enthusiasm for the job in hand was typical of so many voluntary workers in Basildon, particularly in the pioneering years when self-help was often the only way forward.

Although Basildon was generally a town of young people, the O.A.P. movement was very active in the older areas of Laindon, Pitsea and Vange. A leading light in the

55. Mr. John Moyler, a lifelong Salvationist, who did so much in the 1950s to publicise the activities of old age pensioners in the Basildon area.

continual struggle to get a better deal for pensioners was Mrs. Ethel Maddox, who lived in Winifred Road, Pitsea. An executive member of the National Federation of O.A.P. Associations, Mrs. Maddox spent many hours each week visiting pensioners' clubs in her huge area, which covered most of East Anglia. In a campaign to gain support for better pensions she organised a mass procession to the House of Commons in 1950 to lobby M.P.s. In addition to being an active member of her own Pitsea O.A.P. Association branch which met at St Michael's Hall in Rectory Road, Ethel Maddox found time in 1950 to help form five other branches at Canvey, Rayleigh, Southend, Runwell and Tooting.

Mrs. Maddox was a shrewd tactician and was never slow to use even the slightest excuse to gain publicity in the newspapers. Behind her, in this respect, was John Moyler, another O.A.P. champion and salvationist from Laindon who used his training as a journalist with *War Cry* and *The Musician* to flood the newspapers with copy. Both Ethel Maddox and John Moyler did a grand job for the elderly and without them the standing of pensioners in Basildon might not have been so high in later years.

Chapter 7

Basildon: the Ups and Downs

Being the last of the New Towns around London to be given government approval proved a handicap for Basildon because it was never able to enjoy the benefits of low interest rates available in the immediate post-war period. These had enabled the earlier New Towns to carry out large capital development schemes at a crucial time, financed by relatively cheap money. When Basildon needed to attract similar investments the country was caught up in the rising tide of spiralling borrowing rates. Another setback came in 1955 when the government imposed tough restrictions on capital expenditure while Basildon was in dire need of amenities of every sort for its growing population. It took the new town many years to recover from these setbacks.

At first the town's top priority of house building was not affected and, after the completion of the first homes in June 1951, building continued at an ever increasing rate. By the end of 1952 some 600 had been built. Another 860 houses were completed in 1953, 880 in 1954 and from 1955 onwards well over a thousand were built yearly: 1,480 in 1955, 1,350 in 1956, 1,300 in 1957, 1,440 in 1958 and 1,070 in 1959. By 1962 over 13,260 homes had been completed by the Development Corporation alone, increasing the population by nearly 50,000 people.

The building proceeded mainly from east to west in the direction of the proposed town centre, with the two largest housing neighbourhoods of Fryerns and Barstable being the main scenes of operations between 1951 and 1956. By 1956 building had also begun on the main Vange estate and also on Kingswood, immediately south of the town centre. A start had also been made on Lee Chapel South. In 1958, a year when the government demanded greater housebuilding response from authorities all over the country to meet the national target figures, a huge corner was carved out of the area designated for Gloucester Park, for a new housing area named Ghyllgrove. This estate won a government design award, but it was later withdrawn when roofing faults were found which cost many thousands of pounds to repair.

By the end of 1961 Fryerns, Barstable, Kingswood, Lee Chapel South and Ghyllgrove estates were virtually completed and Lee Chapel North was progressing. This then left the Development Corporation to tackle the more difficult redevelopment of the existing villages of Laindon and Pitsea.

Like most New Towns, a wide variety of house types was provided in Basildon. Most homes were of the two- or three-bedroom kind in terraces, but some three-storey maisonettes, one-bedroom flats, bungalows and semi-detached four-bedroom houses were also constructed. To achieve variety, architects used a whole range of materials, colours and textures on the houses and with irregular street layouts providing open aspects of green space, the end result was a pleasing appearance which won Basildon's designers a number of awards and commendations.

In early Basildon the planners provided one garage for every six houses but with the ownership of cars extending much more quickly than anticipated, this ratio soon proved

56. A mixture of the old and new at Vange. In the centre a parade of old shops which served pre-New Town residents in the Bull Road area of Vange is dwarfed by new Corporation houses and flats at what is now the Clay Hill Road junction with Timberlog Lane.

57. Flat-roofed houses on the Ghyllgrove estate at Basildon which won a design award, only for it to be withdrawn when faults were found in the roofs.

58. Early New Town housing in Holden Gardens, Fryerns, when the estates had much more open space and grassed landscaping than today.

59. The first bungalows to be built in the New Town specifically for old age pensioners. These were on the Fryerns estate.

inadequate. From 1957 the corporation increased the ratio to one garage for two houses, but soon afterwards started making provision in new estate plans for one garage per house. The increase in motor vehicles led to the first attempts in Basildon to segregate traffic from pedestrians on the housing estates. The first was in Vange where the scheme was designed by Sir Basil Spence, the famous Coventry Cathedral architect. In later housing areas, particularly at Laindon, much greater attention was paid to segregation, although the price paid was a noticeable increase in densities. Garden space was also reduced in favour of more public open space within the estates themselves.

Experiments were also made with industrialised methods of house construction. Hailed as the answer to the need for quick building methods, the system-built estates in Basildon were not a great success, several of them taking longer to build than conventional brick housing. In the end the Development Corporation admitted defeat and went back to the well tried brick construction.

Concurrently with house building, the Development Corporation pressed ahead from 1950 with the first industrial estate at Nevendon, south of the Arterial Road which was regarded as the northern boundary of the new town. Quick progress was possible on the No. 1 industrial estate, called Cranes Farm, because (unlike later years when numerous properties had to be bought and cleared to allow redevelopment) the area allocated here was mainly farmland.

Opposition to the New Town, led by various branches of the Residents' Protection Association in Laindon, Basildon, Vange and Pitsea, started at a gallop even before any building work began. The main fear of the existing 25,000 residents in 1949 was losing the freeholds of their homes and land, and not being paid enough compensation to buy replacements elsewhere. The majority lived in dread of being forced to live in a rented property on a housing estate. But gradually, as the years went by, many of these original residents either moved away or became resigned to the fact that they had little choice but to take a corporation home. Some even began to relish the prospect of living in a property with modern services like water and electricity.

The compensation and freehold battle was eventually won and by the end of 1953 support for the R.P.A. began to dwindle. But for people like Joe Rolski, chairman of the Vange branch, this was not a disaster. He told his annual meeting that year that without the R.P.A. people would have suffered much greater disruption than had occurred up to that time. 'If we had not fought for the protection of our homes then we would not have been worthy of being called Britons', he said. Having won their fight for people to have freeholds in the New Town area, the R.P.A. continued for many years afterwards not only to oppose redevelopment when they saw fit but mainly to protect members forced to sell out to the Development Corporation.

One of the leaders in this new role was ex-insurance agent Mr. George Ross, a founder member of the Laindon branch, who served the association for 29 years in one capacity or another. For his long service George was honoured by having a road on a private housing development in Langdon Hills named after him. Ross Way provides a permanent reminder of his and the R.P.A.'s efforts.

The biggest disaster which even the Residents' Protection Association failed to halt was the wholesale destruction by the Development Corporation and its agents of virtually all of Basildon's ancient homes, cottages and farmhouses. One by one they were bulldozed, mainly on the pretext that to retain and renovate them was beyond

60. The Allan family playing croquet on the lawn of Luncies Farmhouse where they lived. The Farm was obliterated to make way for the Barstable estate.

the financial resources of the authorities. The result of that policy is that very little of old Basildon remains for present and future generations. The oldest church, All Saints at Vange, and the district's other old churches like St Nicholas at Laindon, Holy Cross at Basildon and St Michael at Pitsea still remain, but the latter has become derelict and unused since the new church of St Gabriel's replaced it in 1964.

Most of Basildon's old farmhouses, like the 14th-century Moat House Farm, which stood south of Holy Cross Church in Church Road, became bulldozer victims, as did dozens of ancient cottages. Of the farms, Brewitts Farm, off Basildon Road, and Hunt's Farm disappeared to make way for Gloucester Park; the 16th-century Frampton Farm, Nevendon, had to make way for the sewage works; Felmores Farm was lost to create Northlands Park and the Felmore estate; Bluehouse Farm gave its site to the Bluehouse community centre at Laindon, while Southfields Farm, Dunton, built in 1710, was demolished to allow part of the Ford Research Centre to be built. One of the district's oldest farms, Cranes Farm at Nevendon, which dated back to at least the 16th century, was destroyed in 1959, but its name is perpetuated in Cranes Farm Road, the major feeder road through the No. 1 and No. 2 industrial estates. As mentioned previously, one historic old house, Oliphants, which in the 1930s became Basildon Rectory, had a life of ups and downs. It was burned down early in the century, rebuilt, badly damaged twice in the last war and then rebuilt again, before being knocked down to make way for Ford's tractor plant.

All the larger properties in Basildon, like the 17th-century Vange Hall, Basildon Hall, the moat of which can still be seen south of East Thorpe and Clickett Hill, and the 15th-century Laindon Hall which was burned down by vandals in 1964, no longer exist. The only two survivors are the 16th-century Chalvedon Hall and Pitsea Hall (c.1600), both at Pitsea.

Chalvedon Hall was in private occupation until 1977 when its last owners, Mr. and Mrs. Peter Croft, sold it to Basildon Council for what today seems a give-away price of £35,000. The main reason for their departure was the high price needed to carry out renovations and preservation. It was a bold decision by the Council to step in smartly to save what was almost the last remaining ancient home in Basildon, although even that was being surrounded by a mushrooming council estate. To ensure Chalvedon Hall was suitably preserved Basildon Council sold the lease of the property with very stringent conditions to a brewery and the old building is now still in use as a public house serving a heavily populated area of the town.

Legend has it that the Hall had a secret underground passage leading to Little Chalvedon Hall in Bowers Gifford, but in fact it headed towards Pitsea Marshes in a southerly direction. The entrance to the tunnel was from behind a cupboard which was boarded up for two centuries after part of the passage collapsed in the 1700s. Chalvedon Hall also had a priest's hole, a small secret room next to the attic. It was built during the reign of Elizabeth I when Catholics were being persecuted and was used to hide their priests. The underground tunnel also gave them an escape route from the building. As with many other old buildings, the Hall was said to have the ghost of a scullery maid who appeared at odd times in the armoury. The last occupants, the Crofts, were never lucky enough to see her but their daughter once claimed to have seen a carriage and four outside her bedroom window.

Basildon's other remaining ancient house, Pitsea Hall, stands on the right-hand side just over the railway crossing in Wat Tyler Way, Pitsea, at the entrance to the Wat Tyler Country Park. It is possible that in the future this old building will be converted for commercial use like its other Pitsea counterpart.

One property not in the same league as the various halls and solid brick farmhouses, but equally famous as part of Basildon's past, was Barstable Cottage, the wooden house pictured so often in books and articles. It stood in Hotwater Lane, now the heart of Basildon town centre, on a site approximately between the escalator in Town Square and Brooke House.

In the early part of the century the Styles family lived there but in 1920 they departed and it became for the next 30 years the home of Walter and Anna James who previously lived in Stepney. They had three daughters, Winnie, Gertrude and Doris, and a son Reg who was born at the cottage in 1925. After marrying, the girls continued to live in Basildon, Gertrude and Doris in properties either side of Fobbing Farm (now St Luke's Hospice) and Winnie, with her husband George Moss in a house called 'The Nest', quite close to Barstable Cottage.

61. Cranes Farmhouse which stood on the site in Cranes Farm Road at Basildon where the first New Town factory was built near the junction with Honywood Road. This was one of Basildon's oldest farms, dating back to the 16th century.

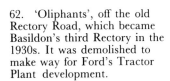

62. 'Oliphants', off the old Rectory Road, which became Basildon's third Rectory in the 1930s. It was demolished to make way for Ford's Tractor Plant development.

63. Chalvedon Hall, Pitsea, one of the few ancient homes in Basildon to survive the New Town. It is now a community public house.

64. The 16th-century Pitsea Hall which stands near the level crossing at Pitsea station. The Hall survived the building of the railway line in the 19th century and also the development of the New Town in the present century.

The first sign of any problem came when plans for Basildon New Town were made public. They showed that both Barstable Cottage and The Nest were right in the middle of the proposed town centre. In 1954 they were eventually taken over by the Corporation, Mr. and Mrs. James being paid only £150 for their home. Most of the money was spent moving them into an old peoples' bungalow in Whitmore Way where the new life on an estate was alien to them both. They hated it. When they became more and more depressed, Mr. and Mrs. James moved to Elm Park to live with a grandson, but it did not last and after a family disagreement they moved to Deal where they both eventually died.

Life in Barstable Cottage was quite primitive. The kitchen had no sink and the water was drawn from a natural spring pumped up by hand. The house had a huge staircase in the middle with two large rooms downstairs and two bedrooms upstairs. Old Mr. James was a very skilled craftsman, completely self-taught, mainly from books. Most of the walls in the cottage were made by him in oak and were beautifully polished and varnished. As well as being a master carpenter, he was also a skilled engineer and an artist, specialising in gold inlay work on books. He also put electric light into the cottage by making his own generator from two diesel bus engines and a set of batteries. It was used in 1949 to power the Jameses' first television set, 'no bigger than a paperback book'.

At one time Mr. James worked as a general maintenance man for a large insurance firm in the City where he carried out a whole range of work from french polishing to decorating. To get to Laindon Station he walked from the cottage along Elizabeth Drive

65. One of old Basildon's best remembered buildings is Barstable Cottage, often featured, with cows grazing in the grounds, in publicity material. This photograph shows the cottage from a different angle with newly-wed Peggy James at the door. Peggy married Reg, the only son of Anna and Walter James, who lived at Barstable Cottage for over 30 years.

66. Ann and Walter James (rear) with son Reg, daughter Gertrude, and Walter's mother (seated) in the garden of Barstable Cottage.

at Laindon, and it took him 45 minutes every morning and evening. In his spare time he kept pigs, goats, chickens and rabbits and cultivated a whole range of vegetables in his garden. He also grew tobacco plants and made his own cigarettes and cigars. His grandson, Tony Moss, remembers it was his job when visiting the cottage to collect the yellow tobacco leaves and to hang them up to dry in a timber shed. At the right time these would be cured and pressed in a big old printing press, ending up as one large jet-black block of tobacco. The old man would then spend hours rubbing it and taking out the veins.

Tony recalled that Barstable Cottage was a very creaky building because it was wooden. Only the fireplace and chimney were of brick. Inside the Jameses had a huge ship's table which was so long that Mr. James was able to walk on it from one end of the room to the other to do the decorating.

One of the saddest things for the family was that, although the cottage had to be vacated in 1954, over two years elapsed before it was demolished. Their son Reg, who died in 1986, found that, even though he had moved out long before, the disruption that his parents suffered was very hard to come to terms with. His wife Peggy, who spent the first three weeks of her married life at the cottage said, 'Reg's feelings ran very deep because an old, very dear way of life had been shattered, causing great distress to his parents. Reg never talked about the cottage after that, but I know he never forgot'.

Many other families in the New Town were equally embittered by losing their homes and the majority had little alternative but to take the accommodation offered to them by the Corporation. The only consolation was that some of the displaced people were given preferential terms for the rented houses. Some were allowed to move into a corporation home rent free for the rest of their lives under a scheme whereby the compensation for their old house was retained in lieu of rent. Another option was a concessionary rents scheme under which people only paid back as rent the interest received on the compensation sum. In other cases people took only part of their compensation pay-off and were charged a lower rent for their new homes. A great number of people took advantage of the various reduced rent offers, although it is true to say that they were introduced in the first place mainly to encourage people to sell out without lengthy and costly negotiations.

The initial reaction of most existing residents was to oppose the New Town and the redevelopment of the area. But by 1955 there was a marked increase in the numbers selling to the Corporation by agreement, without the need for unsavoury compulsory purchase proceedings.

There was also an early indication at the Corporation's Bowers Gifford headquarters that one of the biggest problems they would face would be in tracing the owners of the hundreds of plots of land left undeveloped in the area. This first came to light in the Corporation's annual report of 1956 which disclosed that 106 owners of the 162 land parcels purchased that year could not be traced. Later things got even worse.

For the plotlanders and the week-end bungalow owners, 1958 was a black year which saw 484 homes demolished, most of them in the Lee Chapel North area. A further 219 disappeared in 1959 and 294 more the following year. Those who thought the 1958 demolition figures bad were given a further shock in 1962 when the number of sub-standard properties knocked down broke all records — a total of 618. In the following two years another 750 met the same fate.

The Lee Chapel North experience was the first major redevelopment of a heavily populated area and it involved the removal of some 25 miles of unmade roads, the purchase of 1,000 properties and the planning and building of a completely new housing area with its network of roads and sewers. On the eastern side of Basildon, a start was also made on buying up land at Pitsea. In that part of town, in addition to the Development Corporation, Basildon Council was also deeply involved in negotiations for land for the expansion of council estates east and west of Rectory Road.

While the Corporation were congratulating themselves that most purchases were by now proceeding without appeals to land tribunals, this also showed that people were either generally satisfied with the prices offered for their homes and land, or could not risk appealing for financial reasons. In the first years of the New Town some of the compensation offered to freehold owners was pathetically small. Later these offers became more realistic but there were still many variations which on the surface did not seem justified.

Laindon Residents Protection Association did a great deal of fine work fighting compensation claims and in 1963 they disclosed a case where a bungalow with a large plot of land was sold to the Corporation for only £250. Six years later a 90-acre farm in the same area was sold for £850,000. The reason for the variation was usually the differences in the designation of the land. If owners were lucky enough to have their property on land zoned for housing or industry, they normally received fair prices. If the land was zoned for recreational use, the value plummeted and many found this difficult to understand.

For those living in pre-New Town Basildon, the greatest dread was to receive an envelope marked 'Basildon Development Corporation'. Hundreds did, and for many of them it meant the first stage of being taken over. The chairman of the Residents Protection Association, George Ross, once wrote: 'You read the letter once and then you read it again. Then you suddenly get a funny feeling in the pit of your stomach and you feel sick'. Many people in the Basildon area experienced that feeling.

Chapter 8

The Newcomers' Greatest Needs

Once the new population started to flood into Basildon at a rate of four or five thousand a year, the greatest needs were shops, a hospital, schools and social and recreational facilities within easy reach. Later, when the town centre began to function, a central railway station was added to the list.

The early estates were designed on a neighbourhood principle, each containing a small group of pantry shops, a school, a public house and in later years a community hall, so the everyday needs of most people could usually be met within walking distance. But in the first few years progress seemed very slow indeed. Two small Co-op shops in Pendle Drive, surrounded by a few new homes and a clutter of sand, cement and builders' material, were all the first hundred arrivals in the Fryerns area had on their doorstep for well over a year. Then a second larger shopping parade was built in Whitmore Way, providing a much needed hardware shop, a Post Office, a chemist, a newsagent, a grocery shop run by Home and Colonial, and a fish and chip shop which many of the ex-Londoners appreciated more than anything.

Barstable neighbourhood progressed along the same lines with two small shops opening in Luncies Road before the main Barstable centre was built in Timberlog Lane. Later when estates at Kingswood, Lee Chapel North and Lee Chapel South were under construction, the local shops were opened much earlier for the convenience of the newcomers although at Kingswood and west Fryerns, garages or houses were brought into use as temporary shops while permanent premises were being built.

The first outline plan for the long-awaited town centre was approved by the Ministry in 1956 and engineering work started in December of that year. The first block, of 41 shops, to be started was the one that now faces Basildon market. Within a short time two more blocks of 47 shops at the rear of the bus terminus in Southernhay were begun, and by March 1958 Town Square was beginning to take shape with work pushing ahead on the multiple shop block for Woolworths, Boots, W.H. Smith and the Electricity Board.

The opening, on 16 August 1958, of the first shop in Market Pavement, occupied by a former Laindon tailor and outfitter Mr. Allan Henbest, heralded many such openings over the following years, often performed by celebrities. With the opening on 6 September 1958 of the town centre market and its 50 brightly coloured stalls, people at last could see the heart of their new town beginning to take shape.

By March 1960 some 83 traders were operating in the centre and another 34 shops were ready for occupation. Also completed in that year was the centre's first offices in Keay House, Town Square, two floors of which were taken over by the district council for staff and a council chamber.

By 1961 the town centre was booming and, in one traffic count on a Saturday afternoon, 1,400 cars were parked there at a peak period. The survey also showed that 45 per cent of the cars came from outside Basildon. To meet the demand, extra temporary

67. The first shopping parade to be built in Basildon — in Whitmore Way, Fryerns.

68. Shoppers did not mind the mud in Town Square when the first shops opened in the Keay House block in 1959.

69. The town centre in 1960, with Southernhay sweeping round on the right-hand side, showing the empty-looking bus terminus in front of the South Walk shops, and roads and car parks remarkably free of traffic.

70. The Basildon town centre bus terminus in 1961, looking east.

71. East Square, Basildon, in 1961 with the site on which the Head Post Office was built surrounded by fencing on the left. In the distance work is being carried out on the new Fire Station.

car parks were provided by the Development Corporation but the increased flow of traffic continued always one jump ahead. By December 1963 another count showed 3,000 cars parked in the centre on a Saturday afternoon in the pre-Christmas shopping spree. It all augured well for the prosperity of the centre.

With the town centre's only housing unit, the Brooke House flats, being completed and opened on 7 July 1962 and the Church of St Martin-le-Tours being consecrated in November, further shop development was then slowed down intentionally to allow for consolidation. Attention turned instead towards the provision of necessary public buildings including the Head Post Office in East Square, and the ambulance station, fire station, health centre and police station in Great Oaks.

It was not until 1970 that the centre again began to hum with building activity, work starting on the Marks and Spencer store, Taylor's (now Army and Navy) and Northgate House, as well as the cinemas north of East Square which were eventually opened in September 1971. The completion of the town centre was very much in the forefront of all the Development Corporation's thinking but, with essential major changes in the road pattern, including the diversion eastwards of Southernhay, it was not until March 1980 that the next major milestone was reached — the opening of Savacentre's store at the eastern end of a new covered shopping mall. Within five years the £24 million phase two of the development had been completed and the new covered shopping centre — Eastgate International Centre — opened its doors in November 1985 to an admiring public. It was Basildon's biggest step forward towards the regional shopping centre it had always threatened to become. The only problem was the traffic which it generated; this often brought the town centre to a standstill in the following months.

For Basildon's residents who had struggled through the mud to reach a shop in the early days, Eastgate was like a dream come true. It also became an attraction for people from many miles around, although in 1988 it began to face intense competition from neighbouring Thurrock's huge Lakeside complex. Only time will show whether the two centres can survive in competition with each other.

The Hospital

Possibly Basildon's greatest need in the first 20 years was for a hospital. Being a town with a young population, maternity facilities were essential, but in the beginning the young mothers-to-be had to contend with an awkward bus journey, often in two stages, to get to outpatient services at St Andrew's, Billericay. Facilities at St Andrew's were far from ideal, the complex being made up of a number of old buildings, some previously used as a workhouse, together with a series of Nissen huts which constituted most of the wards.

As early as 1954 the first rumblings of discontent about hospital facilities were publicly voiced in the New Town by the secretary of Basildon Community Association, Mrs. Gladys Taylor. In addition to complaining about the long waiting lists to see specialists in the outpatients' department at Billericay, Mrs. Taylor claimed that the hospital was about 600 beds short of the Ministry of Health's regulations for areas with a population of 120,000 people.

Basildon's M.P., Mr. (now Sir) Bernard Braine raised the issue in the House of Commons, pointing out to the Minister that 4,000 people had moved into Basildon since 1951, making the question of health facilities a matter requiring urgent attention. However, the only joy Basildon got from the Commons was a statement on behalf of the Minister which promised short-term improvements to St Andrew's and Orsett hospitals to bridge the gap before the new hospital was built. In October 1954 a community association delegation went with high hopes to meet the N.E. Metropolitan Regional Hospital Board. They returned with gloomy news that there was 'no hope of a hospital for Basildon in the foreseeable future'. The only good news to come from the meeting was that two more specialists, one for medicine and one for gynaecology, were to be recruited to serve the district.

Fully aware that public opinion could do wonders to force the hospital issue, the tenants and ratepayers' groups, the community associations and the local doctors came together to keep up the pressure. For months, however, there was little sign of progress. Then in August 1955 hope surfaced again when officials from the Ministry of Health and the Regional Hospital Board turned up in the town to visit the site reserved for the hospital. It was the first positive sign of action.

Anxious not to let the pressure relax, petitions containing thousands of signatures were collected and these were backed by Basildon council which added its weight by writing again direct to the Minister of Health. In the meantime pressure continued to mount on St Andrew's at Billericay where, from 2,000 outpatients in 1949, the numbers had risen to an enormous 27,000 by 1955, largely due to the growth of Basildon. In 1957 it was announced that improvements costing £500,000 were to be made to St Andrew's and Orsett hospitals, but in hindsight there is little doubt that this further patching up of the service simply helped to delay the start on the Basildon hospital.

For three years or more progress seemed to be at a standstill and it was not until October 1960 that the anxiously-awaited news was released. During a visit to Basildon, Miss Edith Pitt, the Parliamentary Secretary to the Minister of Health, said that the town would definitely get its hospital and that it was almost at the top of the Ministry's priority list for fund allocation. Then on 26 January 1961 an official announcement in the House of Commons stated that a start would be made on the £2 million hospital in 1964/5. It would have 345 beds, a psychiatric unit and a maternity department.

Later the starting date was put back two years so that the plans could be amended to provide a bigger hospital with 886 beds. A new cost of £5.5 million was announced, although this was later increased to £7 million. The contract was awarded to Sir Lindsay Parkinson who started work on the site on 8 June 1967 when the Lord Lieutenant of Essex, Sir John Ruggles-Brise, cut the first sod.

72.   Basildon General Hospital seen from the air soon after it opened in April 1973.

On 1 April 1973, almost 20 years after the long campaign had started at a tenants' meeting in a builders' hut in Basildon, the new hospital opened its doors to the public. Even so, the casualty department was to remain closed until July 1975, due to a shortage of staff.

Education

Delays in providing enough places in Basildon schools for young children in the New Town in the early years was partly due to the swift influx of new people, and also to the abnormally high birth rate after the war.

When the first tenants arrived in 1951, primary age children were offered places at two existing schools in Vange and Nevendon. At one period Vange Primary School, which at nearly a century old was the oldest in the district, was so overcrowded that some pupils were taught in St Paul's church hall in Timberlog Lane. By 1953 Pitsea Primary School was bursting at the seams with 842 children on the roll, an overflow of 130 pupils. In the same year with the situation becoming ever more critical, 130 children were bussed out of Basildon to schools in Benfleet until places became available locally.

It was not until 29 April 1954, almost three years after the first tenants arrived, that Basildon's first new school, Swan Mead Junior and Infants, opened in Church Road. The junior school headmaster was Mr. Bernard Goodfellow. By that time Basildon's biggest estate at Fryerns was growing fast but it was not until 6 September 1954 that the Whitmore Junior and Infants schools were opened there.

When the school building programme eventually caught up and kept pace with the level of incoming population, bussing children out of the district became a thing of the past. In fact in the late 1960s the situation was reversed, and children from Billericay, Wickford, Thurrock and sometimes Benfleet were brought into Basildon for their schooling. Some of these children attended the two excellent grammar-technical schools at Fryerns and Barstable, which set very high standards from the start under their respective head teachers, Mr. Cyril Baggs and Mr. Geoffrey Whitehead.

In 1961, following several years of pressure from the district council, Basildon became an excepted district for education. This meant that it broke away from Essex's divisional system and was allowed to have its own Committee for Education to take charge of the day-to-day administration of local schools. At the time of the change, Basildon district had 42 schools (34 infant and junior and eight secondary), containing 17,834 pupils. Five of the primary schools were built before 1903. The teacher-pupil ratio at the time was: primary 1 to 37.48 and secondary 1 to 21.80.

Before 1961 Basildon was part of the County Council's S.E. Essex Division under the control of a much respected Education Officer, Mr. F.G.E. (Freddy) Manns. After 1961 Mr. Manns also became Basildon's District Education Officer. Born in Gravesend, Mr. Manns lived most of his life in Essex, entering local government on leaving school at the age of sixteen. He took over as D.E.O. for S.E. Essex at the end of the war and remained in office until his retirement in 1969. Mr. Manns looked on himself as a 'counsellor, adviser and friend' of his head teachers, making it a practice to keep in close touch with them by visiting their schools as often as possible. He once wrote in a booklet compiled by the Confederation for State Education that he always impressed upon his officers that their function was to do everything possible to enable the teachers to do their jobs in the best conditions and circumstances. 'It is a question of educational logistics, of placing the right set of children with the right equipment in the right surroundings', he wrote.

When Basildon took over education functions in 1961 there followed a great deal of talk both in political and teachers' circles about the relative merits of the various

73. Swan Mead Junior School, Vange: recorder group in 1964. Swan Mead was the first new school to be built in the early days of the New Town.

comprehensive systems of education operating mainly in London. Being a forward-looking authority, Basildon decided to research the matter and set up a comprehensive schools commission. For two years this research commission went through the motions and in the process visited schools in London, Leicestershire and elsewhere, but few firm conclusions were reached, and certainly no agreement materialised as a result of the discussions held by the Education Committee. Then in May 1963, the district council elections saw a change to the Labour Party whose pre-election manifesto gave a pledge to produce a comprehensive scheme for Basildon within three months. The electorate gave them the opportunity to do so and the promise was kept.

The chairman of the Education Committee was Councillor Alf Dove, who wrote later in the C.A.S.E. booklet:

The Education Officer Mr. Manns did not know what hit him because we asked him to produce so many plans. We had to consult with everyone and soon found the teachers were very divided on the

74. Staff at Craylands School in Timberlog Lane, *c*.1951. Craylands was Basildon's principal secondary school in the pre-New Town period.

75. Laindon School's football team in 1946/7 when they won the South-East Essex Schools' championship. Headmaster Mr. George Radford is seated left, and at the rear left is Mr. J.H.J. Woodward who succeeded him and later went on to become Head of Woodlands School, Basildon.

matter, some opposing any change at all, others wanting various permutations of different schemes, while others were prepared to go along with us.

Because of the variety of opinions expressed, Basildon decided to take the initiative and to devise a scheme covering the 11-18 age group, but it took a great deal of hard work and many hours of discussion to get it through both the council and the teachers' organisations. Under the final scheme, the old Craylands Secondary School was to be joined with Fryerns Grammar Technical School to make one big Fryerns School. Timberlog Secondary School was to be linked with Barstable Grammar Technical School. The other secondary schools, Nicholas, Laindon and Chalvedon were to stay as they were but run on comprehensive lines, while Woodlands Boys and Woodlands Girls were to remain single-sex schools on the insistence of the Minister of Education.

The chief opposition to the scheme came from those who were reluctant to see the demise of the two highly successful grammar-technical schools, Fryerns and Barstable, which in their short lives had become a credit to the district. There was also a great deal of sympathy for Mr. Victor Robson, the head teacher of Timberlog School, who had built up the secondary school from new into one of the best for miles around. Under the new scheme he seemed certain to be out of a job, and this proved to be the case.

Such was the situation inherited by Mr. Eric Dixon when he took over as Basildon's second (and last) district education officer in 1966. He came from Plymouth where he had been the Assistant Director of Education. Under his leadership the education committee, which was the council's biggest spending committee, made a good job of administering the schools and guiding them through a most difficult transition period into comprehensive education. Education stayed in Basildon's overall control until the next round of local government re-organisation in 1974 when all its functions were returned to county councils where they have remained.

Councillor Alf Dove was a member of the education committee for all its 11 years and was chairman for seven. He said:

> When I became chairman in 1963 there was no regular consultation with anyone. We soon put this right by setting up regular talks with teacher groups and then with parents' organisations.
>
> After 1966 we tried to form a youth consultative committee for children of 14 and over but it did not catch on and we then relied mainly on the youth centres to reach this age group. My one regret is that we never got around to consulting schoolchildren themselves.

Social and Recreation

For a number of years the local schools provided virtually the only venues for dances and similar functions and the first three tiny community huts provided in Fryerns, Barstable and Vange touched only the tip of the iceberg in the increasing demand for venues. Most organisations went out of Basildon for functions such as annual dinners and dances, Southend being the favourite destination because of the good choice of banqueting facilities at the hotels. Those who preferred to stay locally used such places as the *Crown Hotel*, Langdon Hills, the *Railway Hotel*, Pitsea, the Essex Country Club or the Memorial Hall at Laindon, or the church halls.

The first purpose-built community centre to be provided in the Basildon area was at Laindon in 1959, following a magnificent fund-raising effort by Laindon people and a generous donation of £4,000 by Mr. George Sibbons which started the ball rolling.

There was never the same community spirit in Basildon capable of raising such large amounts for leisure facilities and it was left mainly to the county council and grants available from the Ministry of Education to fund the building of Fryerns Community Centre in Whitmore Way which opened in October 1960. It was the first and last such centre to be built in the New Town, other than the replacement of the old Laindon Community Centre in 1988 after a fire which had destroyed the previous building a few years earlier. The new building in the High Road was financed by Basildon Council.

On the last few housing neighbourhoods to be developed by the Corporation it became policy to provide small community halls as a matter of course, as at Kingswood, Lee Chapel North and Lee Chapel South. In the 1970s the Council also embarked on an ambitious programme of providing tenants' meeting halls on many of the estates in Basildon and these became widely used for meetings and the staging of various activities.

From the early days it had been the responsibility of the Council to provide sports facilities and their biggest problems were the high initial cost of the land, and then the cost of overcoming the serious drainage problems of the London clay for outdoor pitches.

The first recreation ground was at Holy Cross, next to the old village church. This was used for soccer and rugby in the winter and cricket in the summer. The development of Gloucester Park was eagerly awaited by the sporting fraternity, but it took a long time to get started due mainly to arguments over financial responsibility. While the politicians continued the debate, hundreds of tons of soil taken from development sites all over Basildon was dumped week by week in the park to form the present attractively landscaped artificial hills south of Cranes Farm Road.

In the late 1960s Basildon Corporation was keen to encourage industry and the various authorities to pull together to form a Basildon sports trust to finance and develop a sports centre in the town park. The idea foundered because of lack of support from the council, and also because the large industrial concerns such as Carreras, Marconi and Teleflex preferred to develop their own facilities for their employees on a less lavish scale than envisaged by the Corporation.

With the annual growth of sports clubs and organisations covering a wide spectrum of activity, a major step forward was taken in 1959 with the formation of Basildon Sports Council, an organisation which went on to be a model for others all over the country. Not only was the Sports Council able to act as a sounding board for the council on all sports matters but it also became a powerful pressure group for more and better facilities. Two of the top priorities were a swimming pool and a running track for the district.

The site for the pool had been earmarked for some time at the town centre end of Gloucester Park, but all the arguments centred around its size, whether it should be Olympic or international. The Sports Council went for the bigger pool for two reasons. They firstly considered the Olympic pool would be needed to cater for the growing population and secondly they saw the prestige value for Basildon of having a venue suitable for staging world-class events. When the discussions first started early in the 1960s there was a difference of some 50 per cent between the costs of the two pools, but by the time the project got off the ground the smaller pool selected by the council cost almost as much as the estimate for the larger one three years previously. The pool was eventually opened on 10 April 1968 and in the end the cost worked out at almost £500,000 including equipment.

The appointment of Mr. David Taylor as the new Town Manager in 1966 looked on

76. The line of Basildon Road in 1957. The right-hand side of the photograph is now Gloucester Park and the first signs of the artificial hills can be seen. Over two million cubic yards of surplus soil was deposited in the park over a period of 10 years to make these hills.

the surface to be a good move for sport as he was known to be a keen sports follower and had expressed support for the sports centre project. Mr. Taylor's stock certainly rose in July 1967 when the council announced plans for a £1.5 million sports centre in Gloucester Park, but after much time, money and effort had been spent in the planning and design the plan was scrapped when the council decided that it had more urgent priorities for its available money. The news came as a stab in the back to both the sporting fraternity and the town manager. So the plan was put on ice and remained frozen for over ten years until a compromise scheme was produced and implemented in the 1980s. This scheme included the provision of two smaller sports centres at Pitsea and Laindon plus some major improvements to the stadium area of Gloucester Park, including a new all-weather running track and training area.

Another sports facility affected by political intervention was the golf course which Basildon Development Corporation planned and designed for the town. The intention from the start was that the course would be a private one, but half-way through its construction Basildon Council intervened and objected to so much open space in the centre of the new town being used 'for an exclusive few'. They took their argument to the Minister for the Environment and he supported the councillors. As a result, the Corporation was forced to change its plans and the course eventually became a municipal one for use by the general public and under the administration of the council. The local authority, however, declined to build the proposed clubhouse and this was left to Basildon Golf Club to provide at their own expense on land leased to them by the authority.

Railway Station

The last of the big campaigns which dominated the 1960s was aimed at getting a central railway station for the town. A site had been earmarked by the presence of an advertising board and a mark on the town centre plan for some years, but progress was very slow. The biggest problem was that at the height of the campaign British Rail, under the direction of Dr. Beeching, was embarking on wide-ranging cost-cutting exercises throughout the country and their policy was to close more stations, not to open new ones.

The Development Corporation had always been very keen on a central station, arguing that it was needed for commuters then relying on the two existing stations at Pitsea and Laindon, and also for the shop owners in the town centre who needed it to bring customers to Basildon and to help staff recruitment. In June 1960 Basildon Town Centre Shop Association collected 5,500 signatures in a petition which was sent to the Minister of Transport. It met with little response.

Nothing was heard for two years after that until the council joined forces with the Corporation in sending a deputation to British Rail in April 1962. At the meeting it was made clear by B.R. that Basildon would only get its central station if the two authorities contributed towards the cost. This demand was slightly amended later in the year to 'a financial contribution to the cost plus the closure of either Laindon or Pitsea stations'. Basildon Council opposed any sort of contribution on the grounds that the station would benefit only a section of their ratepayers. They also claimed that the closure of one of the existing stations would defeat one of the objects of providing the central station.

The problem remained deadlocked for several years before the Development Corporation finally negotiated a scheme to get Basildon its new station without cost to the ratepayers and shopkeepers. Under the plan it had been agreed that the Corporation would allow a developer to build a 271,000 sq. ft. office block alongside the railway line in the town centre in return for financing the building of the station. In April 1971 the £300,000 deal was signed and prospects looked hopeful. Work started on the office block in January 1973 but had still not been completed by the time the station was ready to open to the public on 24 November 1974. It remained empty for some time afterwards and its future looked decidedly bleak until the Ford Motor Company stepped in to take over the whole building in July 1977 as a headquarters for its European truck operations which was to employ 2,000 people. The price which had to be paid for this was the loss of a large public car park south of the railway line which the company wanted for its employees during the week. This proved to have a serious affect later on the public car parking situation in the town centre.

Looking back over the long fights for the hospital, the station, sports facilities and social centres in Basildon, it is clear that very little came easy to the pioneers in the New Town. It was a lesson which was learned by the second and third generations of New Towns which all seemed to make much quicker progress with the provision of such facilities.

In 1989 Basildon New Town celebrated its 40th birthday, yet only a year earlier had the town been provided with a permanent entertainment venue, the new Towngate Theatre. The town's civic centre took even longer: The Basildon Centre was finally completed and opened in November 1989 to provide a home for council staff, a base for essential services, and a home at last for a library in the town centre. Such amenities should never have taken 40 years to materialise.

Chapter 9

Councils, M.P.s and Elections

Before the last war, politics played only a minor role in the life of the Urban District Council compared with the highly organised political groups which existed in the local authority after 1950.

Early in the century Basildon district was administered from Brentwood by the old Billericay Rural District Council which was responsible for a huge area stretching from Brentwood and Herongate in the west to Bowers Gifford in the east. In 1934 the Basildon and Billericay part separated from Brentwood to become an Urban District in its own right, the council offices being moved to No. 108, Billericay High Street where council meetings were held in a room on the first floor.

Most of the 24 pre-war councillors were elderly and most were Conservatives or Independents although they were rarely described in this way. Even on ballot papers at election times only occupations were given after the names of candidates. The first chairman of Billericay U.D.C. was a land and estate agent, Mr. H.E. Bebington, one of the men who during the plotland boom had offered plots in Laindon for sale at £5 a time. He was a Conservative, as was his successor, Mr. Matthew Land, who was chairman from 1936 to 1939. For the next two years Mr. John Ford was chairman, a man described as having 'Labour tendencies'. As there were no council or general elections during the war, casual vacancies were filled by members nominating and voting for replacements. One eminent personality elected this way was Mr. Charles Leatherland (later Lord Leatherland of Dunton) who went on from the U.D.C. to serve on Essex County Council where he became a County Alderman.

During the whole of the war years a leading light on Billericay Council was grocer, Mr. Herbert Harvey, who was vice-chairman for two years from 1939 and then chairman from 1941 until 1946. In this year the council elected its first Labour chairman, Mr. Albert Kaye, a poultry farmer from Basildon who lived in Church Road in a bungalow called 'Enderley' which still exists as the headquarters of the W.R.V.S. Mr. Kaye owned considerable parcels of land in the area now occupied by St Anselm's School.

When the popularity of the Labour Party increased after the war, politics gradually began to play a greater part in the daily life of Billericay Council, and from then on election literature made no secret of the candidates' parties. With the development of the new town at Basildon from 1949, a new-look council began to appear, and the Labour Party gained the odd seat along with some candidates nominated by the anti-New Town Residents' Protection Association. This all led to a much livelier local authority.

Warning shots were fired in the 1952 elections that Labour were becoming a threatening force, and in the following year they won six of the nine contested seats to take control of the council for the first time, with a slender majority of three. Chairman of the council in that first Labour year was Councillor Harry Tanswell, a telephone inspector from Laindon, who was largely responsible for much of the party's growth at

77. In 1953 the Labour Party took control of
Billericay (now Basildon) Council for the first time
and Councillor Harry Tanswell was elected
Chairman. He is seen here receiving the chain of
office from Councillor E. Marchant.

the western end of the town. His vice-chairman was another life-long social-ist and old-towner, Councillor Bill Kiddell, who achieved a long record of service to the district as both a district and county councillor, a school gover-nor and a tireless worker for the com-munity. Labour remained in power for only two years in this first period, but it was long enough for them to plan the council's change of name from Biller-icay to Basildon Urban District Council in 1955 and to set the wheels in motion for the transfer of the council's main offices from Billericay to the centre of Basildon New Town.

The 1955 election proved disastrous for Labour; both Harry Tanswell and Bill Kiddell lost their seats and the Conservatives swept back with a 15-9 majority. But a year later in the May 1956 elections, the two main parties finished level at 13 each, although with the Conservative Brian Edwards in the chair the Tories had the advantage of the chairman's casting vote. This was the first of several such occasions that were later to arise in the council cham-ber at Basildon.

Around this time the Labour Party started to become a very strong political force, particularly through the tenants' associations which were operating on the new estates with considerable success. The associations were supposedly non-political according to their constitutions but they were dominated by socialists (and the occasional Communist) and proved to be very influential on the voters at every election. When Labour regained control of the council for two years between 1957 and 1959, it was the start of a long period of see-saw power control between the Conservative and Labour parties every three or four years.

In 1958 another milestone was reached when for the first time a council meeting was held in the New Town, at Timberlog Secondary School where the hall was converted into a temporary council chamber for the evening. The chairman, Councillor Ted Marchant, presided at that meeting, and opened proceedings by telling the 100 members of the public that it heralded the christening of the New Town as far as civic pride was concerned.

By 1959 the Tories were back in control with a 16-12 majority. Their chairman, Laindon builders' merchant Mr. William Davies, achieved a further landmark by

78. In 1961 Mrs. Christina Gadsdon (centre) became the first woman Chairman of either Billericay or Basildon Council. With her in the photograph are some of the other Chairmen: (left to right) Terry Chapman, Bert Phelps, Baron-Burn, William Davies, Fred Champ, Alf Dove, George French and Brian Edwards.

presiding over a council meeting in a new temporary chamber at Keay House in Town Square where the council's three main departments had moved in March of that year. His vice-chairman between 1959 and 1961 was Wickford councillor Mrs. Christina Gadsdon who in May 1961 became the first lady of either Billericay or Basildon councils to be elected to the chair. Mrs. Gadsdon was also a leading member of the district education committee and a member of the board of Basildon Development Corporation.

When the Conservatives were routed in 1963, partly due to amazing successes by the local Residents Association in Billericay, it started the longest period of Labour control to date, for four years until 1967. This period saw some of the most far-reaching policy decisions to affect the district for the next decades. One was the take-over of a site in Fodderswick, Basildon, for much of the council's administration in 'temporary' offices. They eventually remained there for 25 years during which time a decision to build a permanent town hall was often deferred for both financial and political reasons.

The most important new policy of this period of Labour control was the revolutionary new council administrative system, with a town manager at the helm instead of the traditional town clerk. Most of the committees were reduced to only three members, and the political leader of the majority party became the official Leader of the Council,

79. Councillor Joe Morgan, who was Basildon Council's first Leader, gets a victory kiss from Basildon Carnival Queen Geraldine Gahan who fought him in an election for a Council seat in the Barstable Ward. Geraldine, now a J.P., is mine host at the *Barge Inn*, Vange, which has been run by her family for many years.

80. Basildon's second Town Manager, David Taylor, in consultation with the Council's first Public Relations Officer, David Neaves (left).

a new post. The plan was the first of its kind in the country to be adopted by an urban district council and was the brainchild of the council's first leader, Councillor Joe Morgan and the then Clerk of the Council, Mr. Alma Hatt, who in 1965 was appropriately appointed the first town manager.

Three things hit the plan before it was given a real chance to get off the ground. Firstly, in November 1965 Mr. Hatt collapsed with a heart attack on the day of his appointment and died six days later in hospital. Then, in May 1966, Councillor Morgan's Labour group were defeated in the local elections. The third problem was that just before the elections a new town manager, Mr. David Taylor, had been appointed, partly because of his political credentials as a Labour councillor in Mansfield, Nottinghamshire. This meant that from May 1966 a new Conservative administration found itself half-heartedly trying to administer a new council structure devised by the opposition, as well as having to work with a town manager with opposing political views. It was a situation which led to parts of what was an ambitious and forward-

81. Long-serving Basildon councillor John Potter, who was first elected in 1970, was Leader of the Council when Basildon led the country with a revolutionary charter of rights for its tenants. He is seen addressing a conference on the Charter at the Café Royal in London. Seated is Mr. Chris Holmes who was Director of the National Consumer Council.

looking scheme being considerably diluted in the following months. It all added up to a stormy and uncertain period for the council and not the best of starts for the new town manager. The situation was certainly not helped when in October 1970 the Tory leader Terry Chapman suddenly resigned for personal reasons. For a while the Conservative ranks were in disarray and it came as no surprise when, at the next election in May 1971, Labour swept back into power with a new leader, Councillor Bill Archibald. He remained as leader for a second year in 1972 before handing over to one of the new school of labour councillors, John Potter, who went on to lead the group for the next seven years.

That period included 1974, when Basildon U.D.C. became simply Basildon District Council under national local government re-organisation, with a new town manager, Robin Mitchinson, taking over from David Taylor who took voluntary early retirement. The years from 1971 to 1979 were the longest period without Conservative control of the council running Basildon district. This was partly due to the success of the residents association in the Billericay area which at one time held all nine seats in the town, formerly regarded as a Conservative stronghold. The fact that the majority of the residents councillors were Conservative at heart made no difference to the overall control of the council. With Labour solidly entrenched in most of the New Town wards and the residents' success at Billericay, the council went through a period when a number of pet Labour schemes were pushed through. These included the revival of the development of Gloucester Park, the provision of meeting halls on all council estates, small swimming pools at Pitsea and Wickford, and several big housing developments, mainly at Pitsea and Laindon. Also considered was the development of the marshes area at Pitsea as a country park and conservation area, later to be called Wat Tyler Park.

In May 1979 the swing to the Conservatives both nationally and locally saw Basildon's Tories regain precarious control of the council, but only with the support of the Billericay residents' councillors. Under this arrangement the residents provided a chairman for the first time in the person of Councillor Cliff Jones, and a vice-chairman in Tony Greaves, while the Conservatives were allowed to appoint long-serving Tony Ball as Leader of the Council. Ball held office for three years until in May 1982 Labour sprang back into power for six years, when in a hung council the Conservatives were in charge for just 12 months. This time they had a new leader, building society manager Tony Archer from Billericay who replaced Tony Ball, who had died of a heart attack in October 1987 at the age of 56. The Labour group also elected a new leader when they regained control in 1989. Peter Ballard, an accountant, took over from local government officer Harold Tinworth who had been the Leader of the Council since 1982. Councillor Ballard's biggest task was to steer the district into the new and controversial era of the community charge.

M.P.s and General Elections
Only on very rare occasions in the last 50 years has the political complexion of Basildon Council been the same as the district's Member of Parliament. This has generally not benefited the area. The longest period when the M.P. and the Council at least had the same political label — if perhaps occasionally different points of view — was between

1974 and 1979 when Mr. Eric Moonman was the Labour M.P. and the council was in socialist hands.

In the last century and right up to the end of the last war, Basildon district was part of the large Essex South Eastern parliamentary constituency which included the districts of Basildon, Billericay, Laindon, Pitsea, Vange, Grays, Tilbury and Orsett. From 1885 to 1923 the constituency was consistently in Tory hands, the only break from tradition coming in 1906 when a Liberal, Mr. R.E. Whitehead, captured the seat by 2,060 votes. During the last war the M.P. for the Essex South Eastern constituency was a Conservative barrister, Mr. (later Sir) Victor Raikes who was first elected in 1931. He retained the seat with a slender majority of 970 in 1935. With no elections during the war he remained the district's M.P. until July 1945 when for only the third time the constituency elected a Labour candidate, Mr. Ray Gunter, with a majority of 3,591 votes. (The two previous Labour wins came in 1923 — P.C. Hoffman with a majority of 1,600 — and in 1929 when J.R. Oldfield was successful by 626 votes.)

For the 1945 election the South East Essex constituency was reorganised, losing the Grays and Tilbury area, and gaining Canvey Island, Benfleet, Rochford, Rayleigh and part of Southend. It was still like this in 1950 and 1951 when in two successive elections Bernard Braine, later to become Sir Bernard and father of the House of Commons, took the seat for the Conservatives. This was an important period for Basildon because in 1951 the first tenants had started to move into the New Town and they had plenty of grumbles about services provided by the government-appointed Development Corporation. The old towners were just as disgruntled, although in their case it was over the poor rates of compensation being paid for their homes and land.

In 1955 the constituency boundaries were changed again, the districts of Canvey, Benfleet and Rochford breaking away to form a new S.E. Essex constituency. Bernard Braine went with them. In the reshuffle a new-look Billericay constituency was formed, consisting of the whole of Basildon and Brentwood districts. The first Member for that new constituency was Richard (now Sir Richard) Body who in the 1955 election took the seat with a majority of 4,000 votes. The total electorate at this time was 58,872. For the general elections in 1959 and 1964, Richard Body moved elsewhere and the seat was retained for the Tories by the very popular Mr. Edward Gardner, Q.C. But nothing is certain in politics and in 1966 Mr. Gardner was unseated in a fiercely contested election by Labour's Eric Moonman, who was returned with a narrow majority of 1,642 votes.

By the next election in 1970, Mr. Gardner had found a safer seat and Mr. Robert McCrindle was named as the Conservatives' candidate to oppose Moonman. He proceeded to turn the previous result upside down, winning the seat by some 4,000 votes. By February 1974 the name of the constituency had been changed from Billericay to Basildon, and Eric Moonman returned to reclaim his seat in the House with a huge 11,000 majority. He repeated the process with a majority of 10,551 in another general election in October 1974.

By 1979 Basildon's electorate had risen to 103,596 and in the election of that year the constituency went along with the Thatcherite landslide throughout the country and swept the controversial Harvey Proctor into the Commons with an exceptionally large Tory majority of 5,180 votes. The result surprised most of the pundits and even Proctor himself. The issue which possibly made the biggest contribution was the Conservatives'

82. Bernard Braine at a Laindon fête in 1953 when he was M.P. for Billericay (including Basildon).

election pledge to allow more council and corporation tenants to buy their rented homes. With so many of Basildon's population living in this sort of accommodation, many tenants voted for the policy and not so much for the political party. It gave Proctor tail-wind assistance across the threshold into Westminster.

Before the next general election in 1983 there was yet another boundary re-organis-ation; Basildon now included 95 per cent of the New Town area, and Billericay constituency was re-constituted to cater for the towns of Wickford and Billericay, together with a piece of Laindon and a small section of Thurrock. Harvey Proctor chose the safer option and moved to Billericay where he was returned with a majority of 14,615 over his nearest rival, the Liberal Mr. P.M.A. Bonner. In Basildon, Labour's Julian Fullbrook started as an odds on favourite for the seat, but in one of the biggest surprises of the election a new name, David Amess, scored a famous victory for the Conservatives by 1,379 votes. Like Harvey Proctor in 1979, Amess could hardly believe his luck and without a prepared speech he was for once almost lost for words when the result was declared at Basildon's Festival Hall. Amess went on to make it two in a row by winning again in 1987 (Amess 21,585; Fullbrook (Lab.) 19,209; R. Auvray (Lib.)

83. Basildon's M.P. from 1959 to 1966, Mr. Edward Gardner Q.C., with the then Prime Minister, Sir Alec Douglas Home, and Council Chairman, Percy Saunders, in Basildon town centre.

84. Mr. Eric Moonman, who, between 1966 and 1979, was three times a victor and twice a loser when he stood as a Parliamentary Labour candidate in Basildon.

9,139), while at Billericay, in spite of the problems caused by the resignation of Harvey Proctor just before the election, after a scandal which had been brewing behind the scenes for months, the Conservatives held on to the seat. Success went to Mrs. Teresa Gorman — a stranger to most of the constituency only a matter of weeks before the election — who romped home by polling a massive 33,741 votes against the SDP's 15,755 and Labour's 11,942.

Mention the name Billericay in conversation almost anywhere in the country and people's minds go back to the 1950s when twice in succession the Billericay constituency was the first in the country to declare its general election result. In fact the Billericay result was often regarded by commentators in pre-computerised days as the pointer for the final result, as well as for the overall swing from one party to another. The two fantastically quick counts of 67 minutes in 1955 and 59 minutes in 1959 were due to a military style counting operation masterminded by Billericay's Returning Officer and Council Clerk, Mr. Alma Hatt. In his view it was very much a matter of prestige for the district to be first, and to get there he planned his count down to the very last detail. Even reserve cars followed those carrying ballot boxes to the count in case of a breakdown. His counters were also hand picked and specially trained, most of them coming from local banks. The greatest threat to the early declaration bid in 1955 was the widespread nature of the Billericay constituency and the fact that some of the polling stations were 12 miles from the venue of the count. The electorate of 58,872 was not small either.

Hatt's plan was to get the 96 ballot boxes back to the count as speedily as possible following the closure of the polls at 9 p.m., and on the night 78 had been checked in by 9.18 p.m. By 9.23 all were safely in and the counting of the votes was well under way. Pressure mounted in the hall as 10 p.m. was reached and passed but seven minutes later it was all over and television screens throughout the country flashed up the result, a win for barrister Richard Body at Billericay.

After showing the nation that Billericay was first nationwide, Returning Officer Hatt and his assistant Joyce Norris, who went on to become one of the top election experts in the country, set out a new plan to beat the 10 p.m. barrier at the next election in 1959. On the surface this looked an almost impossible task not only because the size of electorate had increased in four years by another 20,000 voters, but because the count was made that much more complicated by the untimely intervention of a third candidate, compared with two at the previous election.

Although a 10 p.m. result was always the talking point among the media, Mr. Hatt secretly thought he could complete the whole counting operation in 50 minutes 'with a little luck and a following wind'. The 400 people involved in the count were keyed up and equally keen to get the quick result, but the odd unexpected hiccup occurred and Mr. Hatt's dream never came true. In spite of this Billericay was first again when the result was declared after 59 minutes by the High Sheriff of Essex, Major G. Benyon Hoare. The time was a record.

After that Billericay became synonymous with quick election counts and, for the election in 1964, reporters from television, radio and the national press descended on the constituency in their hordes both during the campaign and on election day. With everyone expecting Billericay to make it three in a row the count fizzled out like a damp squib and the result was not announced until 11 p.m., almost an hour overdue. The

85. The 1959 General Election count at Billericay was completed in 59 minutes and was the first result in the country to be declared. The count was masterminded by Town Clerk Mr. Alma Hatt (left) and assistant Joyce Norris (in front of microphones), who went on to become an election expert in her own right.

main reason for the failure was Labour's demands for two recounts due to the closeness of the contest, but below the surface a complaint had festered in some quarters that Mr. Hatt was sacrificing accuracy for speed at the counts. Those with this view were anxious to make their point, and they did — at Billericay's expense in front of the whole country.

Whatever the cause, it was the last time Mr. Hatt was given the chance to go for an all-time record which would never be beaten, because by the time of the next election in 1966 he had tragically died. In any case, by that election Billericay's electorate had risen to a massive 102,198, making a quick count so much more difficult. The 59-minute count achieved in 1959 has never been beaten, although Torbay (Devon) came very close in 1987 by declaring its result in 60 minutes. In that same year Basildon's Returning Officer Robin Mitchinson encouraged another attempt at a fast count for the Basildon result, but the engine was not so well oiled as before, although a most creditable third place in the whole country was achieved.

Chapter 10

Civic Offices and Council Officers

Over a period of 60 years from 1930, only six men have held the posts of either Town Clerk or Town Manager in the local councils administering the district covering Basildon New Town. Until 1934 the old Billericay Rural District Council had a Brentwood solicitor, Mr. Charles Lewis, as its Clerk. He remained in charge until the council changed its name to Billericay Urban District Council in 1934 when Mr. Alfred Cheshire was appointed. He stayed for 10 years and then handed over in 1944 to an ambitious new Clerk, Mr. Alma Hatt, the son of a Tilbury docker and previously Deputy Clerk of Thurrock Council.

While at Billericay Mr. Hatt studied for his law examinations and eventually qualified as a barrister. He brought a new lease of life to the council although his

86. Basildon Council Chairman Harry Tanswell greets Alma Hatt and his wife Grace at a Council civic function in 1954.

appointment did not go down well with at least two other senior officers — finance chief 'Lofty' Cousins and surveyor Harry Mayhew — who both wanted the job. Right from the start Mr. Hatt was keen to take the council to the public and he broke all tradition by organising some council meetings in local halls, including the Rose Hall in Chapel Street, Billericay, and also at the local courts. He continued with this policy in Basildon in the early years of the New Town, taking full council meetings to venues in the town and putting the council on show to the public in various 'Question your Council' sessions all over the district. In addition to bringing the New Town to Basildon and becoming a nationally-known expert on elections, Mr. Hatt also had a vision of improving and updating Basildon Council's administration in such an effective fashion that other authorities all over the country would want to imitate it.

The opportunity to put forward some of these ideas came after the 1963 district council elections when an ambitious Labour group took control of the council. It was the year when a genuine new towner in Councillor Alf Dove was elected chairman of the authority for the first time. The group discussed in private some revolutionary schemes, one of which was a complete restructuring of the council administration. It was a particular hobby horse of Councillor Joe Morgan, a tough talking new towner who had come originally from Canning Town. Mr. Hatt saw much of his own thinking in Labour's plan and he and Morgan burned midnight oil for many months putting together a scheme they believed was unique for an urban district council.

The key to the whole idea was the appointment of a council overlord — a Town Manager with chief executive status — to head the council's administration team. He would replace the traditional town clerk who had been the chief officer in councils everywhere since Victorian times. The designers of Basildon's new plan wanted the high powered town manager to function very much on the lines of a managing director in a multi-million pound business. They saw him relieved of all the minutiae which had accumulated over the years, leaving him to deal with only major matters of policy and planning for the future. The town manager would be the chief of the council's chief officers leading a streamlined administration 'more in keeping with the needs of the 20th century' than the old structure.

The new plan provided the council with a cabinet-style policy committee chaired by the Council Leader — a newly created post — and made up only of majority group members. As one of the main instigators of the plan, Councillor Morgan became the council's first leader and took responsibility for getting the scheme off the ground. The plan was a bold and imaginative one which when implemented in 1965 attracted a great deal of publicity in the national and local press and also on radio and television — for Basildon, Mr. Hatt the first new Town Manager, and for Mr. Morgan. But tragedy struck almost immediately when Mr. Hatt died of a heart attack at Guy's Hospital in London only days after his appointment. Three months later the council was forced to go through the whole selection process again to find a new Town Manager. Over 180 people applied for the post and 10 were shortlisted and interviewed over a hectic two days. In the end it came down to two candidates: the council's existing engineer and surveyor, Mr. S.A. Wadsworth, and David Taylor, the National Coal Board official from Mansfield. Taylor won.

A Geordie and ex-miner, Mr. Taylor, at 46, was a product of Ruskin College, Oxford, where he studied on a mineworkers' scholarship before joining the Coal Board in an administrative capacity. Promotion came quickly for him and he became an industrial relations officer with the Board at Mansfield, Nottinghamshire. While there he served as a socialist member of the local council. From managing 18,500 miners in Mansfield, David Taylor found himself in March 1966 as boss of a small chief officer team in local government in Basildon. Some of these officers did not greet his arrival with a great deal of enthusiasm, partly because of his limited local government administrative experience and in two cases because they had wanted the job for themselves.

Taylor had hardly settled into the town manager's seat when the May elections of 1966 saw the Conservatives sweep back into control of the council. They stayed there for the next five years. During this period Basildon was in the difficult position of having a socialist town manager anxious to create an impression and make a name for himself, serving not the Labour administration which appointed him, but a Conservative one. It was an explosive situation. He faced an unenviable task and he inevitably lost a few friends on the way among all shades of opinion. It was not always his fault, but it led eventually to his downfall.

While he was town manager, Taylor was responsible for establishing Basildon as one of the key areas of local government in the country in the various schemes put forward to the Government for the reorganisation of local councils in 1974. Basildon and David Taylor favoured splitting the country into 19 big administrative regions each catering for a population in excess of 500,000 people. In South-East Essex they saw Basildon being the administrative centre of a heavily-populated North Thameside area, which in addition to Basildon would include Castle Point, Southend and Thurrock. In rateable value terms it would have been one of the richest areas in the country because of the Thameside industry and oil refineries in Thurrock together with the growing industrial estates in Basildon New Town. In the end Basildon and Taylor lost the fight to make Basildon one of the local government leaders in the country and the town council ended up virtually as it was before — a district council of 46 members administering an area of almost unchanged size. An additional disappointment was that Basildon even lost some of its former responsibilities including education which, by government direction, went back lock, stock and barrel to the Essex County Council.

Many town clerks throughout the country were made superfluous as a result of the reduction in the number of local authorities, and early retirement on favourable terms was offered to those prepared to go voluntarily. It was no surprise when David Taylor took this option for early release and he bowed out from the council, although not from Basildon, at the end of March 1974. After his retirement David lectured extensively on local government before standing for a Basildon seat in the Essex County Council elections under a Labour ticket. He won the seat but before his four-year term at County Hall was up, he unfortunately died in 1980 after a short illness.

The new man at the helm as town manager for Basildon Council was Mr. Robin Mitchinson, previously Town Clerk at Haverhill in Suffolk and a man who started his local government career in Africa. The council had not found it easy to find a suitable replacement for David Taylor and Mitchinson was very much a candidate who entered the contest at the eleventh hour and captured the post. A barrister and a skilful negotiator, Mitchinson headed a new-look council team which included six divisional officers — a mixture of experience and new young blood. His greatest test of strength in his first months of office concerned the crisis which hit Basildon when news leaked

87. Basildon's third and longest-serving Town Manager Robin Mitchinson (centre) was appointed in 1973 and remained until 1989. The photograph shows him carrying out his favourite public relations role on the Council's publicity stand at the Essex Show. Mr. Godfrey Nhemachena, Town Clerk of the Council's twin town of Gweru in Zimbabwe, is on the right.

88. Councillors join the public in protest against toxic waste dumping at Pitsea in Basildon town centre in 1977.

from the County Council that the amount of toxic waste being dumped at Pitsea's private waste tip had rocketed, sparking off fears about safety to those living in the area. Basildon Council was also concerned about the quantities of liquid waste coming to Pitsea by road from all over the country and as far away as Scotland.

As a result of the council's campaign, led by Mitchinson and council leader John Potter, the waste tip uproar hit the national media headlines and led to an inquiry by a select committee of the House of Commons. The campaign raised Mitchinson's stock locally, particularly as a publicity front man for the council, a role he always carried out with distinction whether on television, radio or in the press, until his departure in June 1989 after 15 years' service. Within a month of leaving, Mr. Mitchinson headed off to Africa to become town clerk of Blantyre in Malawi, the town where he had originally begun his local government career more than two decades earlier.

Mr. Mitchinson's departure caused a great deal of speculation about his successor. In the end Mr. John Rosser's appointment was a popular choice with the staff. A lawyer, he was one of the council's area directors and formerly manager of administrative and legal services, and his initial task was to move the council into their first permanent home, in the Basildon Centre in November 1989. The Centre cost in excess of £18 million at a time when expenditure cuts were more often the rule, and it consequently provided a great deal of ammunition for those who opposed it. The need for permanent accommodation for administrative staff had been keenly felt for nearly 55 years since the old Billericay Rural District Council became an urban district council in 1934 and had moved from Brentwood to 'temporary' offices in High Street, Billericay. As the staff increased, the council had taken over various buildings in the High Street and it soon became obvious that a purpose-built town hall was the only satisfactory solution. With this in mind a site of four acres was purchased before the last war at the corner of Dunton Road and High Road, Laindon. The war halted progress on this scheme and when Basildon New Town came along it became clear that the intended site was most unsuitable for the civic offices and it was eventually sold off to the Development Corporation.

The council's change of name to Basildon from Billericay in 1955 and the move into temporary offices in Keay House in Town Square, Basildon in March 1960, led to further thoughts on the subject. A site of three acres was agreed and bought from the Development Corporation for £30,000, and in January 1961 the council announced that the centre would be designed by the famous Coventry Cathedral architect, Sir Basil Spence and built within five years. Various designs were drawn up in the following few years but little progress was made; in 1965, with Keay House bursting at the seams with the growing number of staff, the council put up a rabbit warren complex of temporary wooden offices on a site owned by the Corporation in Fodderwick in Basildon town centre.

Thanks to the council's foresight in the 1950s the adjacent civic centre site was still available and in council ownership, but progress on its development was delayed firstly by news of possible changes in the Corporation's town centre plan and later by talk of the major reorganisation of local government in 1974. Rightly, the council did not wish to go ahead with an office complex which might be too large or too small for the needs of a reorganised authority. But even after the new councils came into being in 1974, the town hall question continued to take a back seat until 1979. This time the plan was to link the offices with a new theatre and to finance civic amenities partly from the letting of commercial offices on the site. The plan may have been ambitious, but the electorate were unimpressed and pitched the Labour Party and their plan out of office in the May elections which brought a swing to the right across the country.

For the next three years the town hall question led to much talk but few constructive decisions until 1982 it again became a priority and eventually, after a great deal of political wrangling, the scheme was given the go ahead in 1986. Although marred by teething problems, the new Towngate Theatre opened in 1988, an exciting amenity for the town, followed by the opening of the civic complex, the Basildon Centre, in November 1989. The whole project had been dogged by arguments over expenditure both at council meetings and in certain sections of the media. At one stage the whole scheme was in danger of being halted even though several million pounds had already been spent on development work by the contractors. Arguments over the cost and its effect on the pockets of residents will no doubt continue, but the opening of the Centre gave a considerable boost to Basildon's prestige, and the provision of a permanent home for most, if not all, of the council's employees was indeed an historic occasion.

Chapter 11

Basildon Development Corporation

Faced with the formidable task of transforming Basildon into what they hoped would become the best New Town in southern England, Basildon Development Corporation had to contend with a variety of problems. Yet on the whole, most will agree that they generally made a good job of it. In the early years, following the Corporation's creation in 1949, the authority gave an outward impression of aloofness, partly due to the fact that most board members were strangers to Basildon and its people. The situation was also not helped by headquarters established in the east of the district, out of easy reach of most of the new residents and even outside the boundary of the New Town designated area.

Not a great deal of attention was paid to public consultation in those early days and very often the Corporation's only contact with those who opposed redevelopment was at the instigation of the protesters, and then it was often only with lower grade officers. Thankfully, as the years passed, the Corporation became much more attuned to the need for good public relations and certainly in the last 20 years of its life could rarely be accused of keeping its plans for Basildon hidden from view.

Being a government-appointed body, the Corporation's policies over its 37 years were always controlled to a very large degree by politicians in Whitehall, through the Department of the Environment. Not only did the government through the Minister make appointments to the board but it also dictated the direction of the Corporation's policies. The sale of Corporation homes to tenants was an example of a government's wishes becoming a directive to New Town Corporations. In Basildon record sales were achieved following Mrs. Thatcher's victory in 1979 while at the same time the construction of further homes for rent gradually came to a halt. This was in complete contrast to the days of Labour governments under Wilson and Callaghan when council house building was encouraged.

One of the biggest grumbles about the Corporation was the lack of representation on the board not only of experienced local people but of genuine representatives of the new tenants. For many years Basildon Council argued that they should be entitled to at least one representative on the Corporation board even if the place was provided without the customary remuneration paid to members. It was only in the final 10 or so years of the Corporation's existence that it became recognised that the Leader of the Council, regardless of political party, should serve on the board. Councillors John Potter, Harold Tinworth and Tony Ball were all given Corporation seats in this way.

After preparing Basildon's first master plan, the Development Corporation took very early steps in 1951 to attract employers to Basildon to provide work for the town's new tenants, but progress was slow. This was partly due to the fact that Basildon had to compete with the seven other New Towns around London, most of which already had a head start. Basildon's first new factory, opened in 1951 in Cranes Farm Road and owned by South-East Essex Wholesale Dairies Ltd., heralded the first progress on the industrial front. The £25,511 factory was soon followed by others including premises for Rotary Hoes, Marconi Wireless Telegraph Company, the Freedman Upholstery Company, Nufloor Limited and the Ford Motor Company. Other new factories were for Bonallack & Sons and Darham Industries Ltd.

Basildon Corporation were always conscious of the fact that the encouragement of industry to the town was a top priority and by 1960 there was much brighter news on the industrial front; No. 1 estate was almost full and the plans for the No. 2 (Pipps Hill) estate were well under way. After that, Basildon was never too desperate again for industry and that is reflected in the overall success of the later industrial areas, including Burnt Mills, Southfields, Laindon North and Laindon South.

Basildon's worst period, when employment hit a record low, was in the early 1980s and was largely the result of the difficult economic situation which faced the country and not only Basildon. Some 5,060 people were unemployed in Basildon in 1980 and the figure was far too high for what was supposed to be a thriving new town in the prosperous south-east of England. But worse was to come, and in 1984 the unemployment figure reached an all-time high of 10,000 people. One of the main causes for the leap in the figures was the closure of one of the town's biggest employers, Carreras Rothmans, when over 1,500 people lost their jobs. This was due only in part to the economic situation and more because of the national drop in cigarette sales as people gave up smoking for health reasons.

The Corporation had to pull out the stops to attract more employment and they did this by continuing to build their industrial estates, particularly at Southfields in Burnt Mills, with units which could be easily adapted for any need. The policy was a success. They also worked hard to attract investment to the town and in this respect they achieved particular success, with schemes worth an investment figure in excess of £80 million in 1985. The authority also pinned its hopes on the town centre expansion to help the employment situation.

In its 37 years the Development Corporation was served by seven chairmen and only four general managers. The chairmen were: Sir Lancelot Keay (1949-54), Lieut. General Sir Humfrey Gale (1954-64), Sir John Macpherson (1964-67), Mr. William Balch (1968-71), Mr. Arthur Kelting (1971-9), Sir Reginald Goodwin (1979-80) and Dame Elizabeth Coker (1981-6). It was during the chairmanship of Mr. Kelting, a successful businessman, that the first steps were taken to sell off Basildon's assets in preparation for the eventual winding up of the Corporation. Also it became a priority of Mr. Kelting and his board to press ahead with all speed with the completion of the town centre development, including the exciting Eastgate project.

In 1979 Dame Elizabeth Coker was appointed to the Corporation after a distinguished period in local government as a county councillor. Formerly a schoolteacher, she started her county career elected to a Basildon ward, and went on to become not only chairman of Essex County Council, but also of the Association of County Councils and a leading member of Essex's education committee. Under Dame Elizabeth, the Corporation's house building came to a halt in line with government policy and private house building stepped up as prime sites in the south-west corner at Langdon Hills and at Pitsea were sold off to developers. One of the results was that expensive housing was built at Langdon Hills attracting owners who 10 years earlier would never have considered Basildon as a place to live. Another feature of the last years of the Corporation

89. The first factory to be built in Basildon was for the South-East Essex Wholesale Dairies Ltd. It opened in Cranes Farm Road in 1951.

90. The Carreras Rothmans factory in Christopher Martin Road, Basildon, which closed in 1984 with the loss of 1,500 jobs — a blow to the economy of the New Town.

91. The last Basildon Development Corporation board under the chairmanship of Dame Elizabeth Coker pictured in 1986. The officers of the Corporation are on the left.

92. Mr. Charles Boniface (right) was General Manager of Basildon Development Corporation for 21 years. He is seen in this photograph talking to Finnish local government representatives on a visit to a Basildon housing estate.

under Dame Elizabeth was the wholesale selling off of other assets including shops, factories and building sites to private enterprise. This continued until the Corporation was wound up in 1986, the process then being handed over to the Commission for New Towns who followed the same policy, not always to Basildon's best advantage.

Of the Development Corporation's General Managers, the first, Brigadier W.G.D. Knapton, served from 1949 to 1954; Mr. Charles Boniface for a record 21 years from 1954 to 1975; Air Commodore Allen Mawer from 1975 to 1978 and Mr. Douglas Galloway for seven years from 1979 until the end of the Corporation in 1986. Mr. Galloway, who then became the Commission for New Towns' Executive Manager in Basildon until his retirement in 1988, had been associated with Basildon since the early 1950s, firstly as an architect with the Corporation and then as Chief Architect Planner. While in the latter post he was responsible for the planning of 10,000 homes in Basildon, five of the schemes winning design awards. Mr. Charles Boniface joined the authority shortly after it was formed as its solicitor. He was an outstanding leader and most of the decisions which shaped the future of Basildon were made during his 26 years at Gifford House.

Reference was made earlier to the way the Corporation's decisions were often influenced by instructions from Whitehall and there were occasions when some decisions were taken in London without any consultation with the local board. One such was the allocation of a green belt site in Basildon for the building of the Ford Motor Company's big tractor plant.

The story was made public by Douglas Galloway at a presentation party given for him on his retirement in 1988. He revealed that Ford were so anxious to have the Basildon site that the head of the Ford empire, Mr. Henry Ford in person, flew over to London to negotiate directly with government ministers. According to Mr. Galloway, the reason for such high-level intervention was that the government wanted the plant to be located in the North of England rather than Basildon, while Ford wanted to stay in the south. As a result of the meeting with Henry Ford, permission was given direct by the minister, and Basildon Corporation were ordered to comply. They were told to make a formal application within 24 hours for permission to build the plant, in spite of the fact that the go-ahead had already been given. As history has since shown, the tractor plant was built and opened in 1963 on the 100-acre site in Cranes Farm Road, costing Ford £600,000. Since then the factory has made a huge contribution to employment in the town and to the country's export figures.

Chapter 12

Royal and Famous Visitors

Basildon New Town celebrated its 40th birthday in 1989, an occasion worthy of a Royal visit which did not materialise. Several members of the Royal family have graced the town with their presence in those 40 years, but the most notable exception has been Her Majesty the Queen. Is she being saved for the half century celebrations?

The first major Royal visit occurred as far back as 27 June 1957 when the Duke and Duchess of Gloucester spent a day in the town. During the visit the Duke cut a ribbon to open the main town centre road, Southernhay, and also officially named the town main park Gloucester Park. When the ceremony took place the only indication of the park's position was a banner strung up between two trees reading 'Town Park'.

His Royal Highness Prince Philip made the first of his two visits to Basildon on Friday 4 March 1960, the main purpose being to throw a switch at the Carreras cigarette factory in Christopher Martin Road to complete the total automation of cigarette making — the first operation of its kind in the world. After leaving the factory, the Prince also went to the town centre where he met a number of members and officers of both the Development Corporation and the council. He also renewed acquaintance with Basildon resident Bill Freeman who was his orderly on H.M.S. *Whelp* during the war.

Four more years passed before the next royal visit from H.M. Queen Elizabeth the Queen Mother, who landed in the brilliant red royal helicopter in Holy Cross recreation ground off Church Road. Her main mission was to open a new retirement home for the Printers Pension Corporation in Great Spenders called Southwood Court. President of the charity in that year was Sir Billy Butlin of holiday camp fame. The Duchess of Kent was the next royal visitor on 9 October 1968 when she dedicated the new £4,000 porch and a modern sculpture of Christ at St Martin-le-Tours church in the town centre. The sculpture was the last completed work of Mr. Adrian Huxley-Jones who died a few months later.

Apart from flying visits by Prince Philip in 1982 to the Essex County Council's young enterprise centre on the Burnt Mills industrial estate and by Princess Anne to the Ford Tractor Plant in 1989 to mark the plant's 25th birthday, Royal visits to Basildon have been few considering the impact of the New Town on the Essex scene since 1949.

Most of the Prime Ministers of the period, including Harold Macmillan, Harold Wilson, James Callaghan, Sir Alec Douglas Home and Edward Heath, have enjoyed hospitality in Basildon, together with a whole host of government ministers and different party leaders and officials.

One of the most exciting projects to attract VIP attention in the town in the last decade, other than the opening of the Eastgate Centre, was the creation by Basildon Council of the Wat Tyler Country Park on a marshland and rubbish tip area in Pitsea. Former T.U.C. General Secretary Len Murray opened the park on 14 April 1984, dedicating it 'to the memory of those people of Essex and Kent who in the cause of liberty took part in the Peasants' Revolt in 1381'.

93. H.R.H. the Duchess of Gloucester during a visit to Basildon in 1957. She is followed (right) by Lieut. General Sir Humfrey Gale, the Chairman of Basildon Development Corporation.

94. H.R.H. The Queen Mother with the late Sir Billy Butlin at Basildon in 1964 when she opened retirement homes for printers and their families.

95. The Duchess of Kent on a walkabout in Basildon town centre in October 1968 after dedicating St Martin's church porch and sculpture.

96. Mr. Adrian Huxley-Jones working on his sculpture of Christ which he made for St Martin's church in Basildon town centre. He died a few months after the work was unveiled.

97. Olympic walker Johnny Webb leads a training session of budding Basildon walkers on the Gloucester Park athletics track.

98. Basildon's Olympic diver, Alison Drake, with the illuminated address which Basildon Council presented to her in honour of her achievement in 1973. The award was handed over by Council Chairman John Costello.

In sport, Basildon has a proud and outstanding record of achievement, producing over the years a number of top international performers, including boxer Terry Marsh, walkers John Webb and Olly Flynn, runners Eamonn Martin and Matthew Yates, Olympic diver Alison Drake, and England netball captain Jillean Hipsey, as well as many national and county champions across a range of the less fashionable sports from gymnastics to wrestling and windsurfing.

But for two years in the 1980s which included Marsh's sensational world championship win on home territory in 1987 and the arrival a year earlier of an American boxing entourage which included the world's greatest ex-heavyweight champion of all time, Muhammed Ali, it was boxing which took up most columns of publicity for the town in local and national newspapers. The appearance of Ali — a shadow of his former confident self — was a supporting act in July 1986 to the Tim Witherspoon circus which descended on Basildon to prepare for the American's world heavyweight title fight with Frank Bruno at Wembley. The Witherspoon camp took over the *Crest Hotel* which was conveniently situated next door to the Festival Hall where Witherspoon's training sessions were held. Nothing was left to chance to keep the party happy and the hotel even had to order specially-made large beds to accommodate the champion and some of his lofty sparring partners. It is now history that Witherspoon won the contest by stopping the popular Bruno, after which the entourage and hangers-on returned to Basildon, where the celebrations went on for several days. Eventually, hotel manager Stuart Coney breathed a sigh of relief when the party finally bade farewell, leaving behind many happy memories and new-found friends.

All the excitement of that occasion paled into insignificance, however, when in a circus marquee on a car park in March 1987, local fireman Terry Marsh became Basildon's first ever world champion. On a night charged with emotion and in front of 5,000 excited supporters, Marsh captured the world light welterweight crown by stopping the American holder of the title, Joe Manley, in the tenth round amidst scenes of pandemonium watched by thousands on television. The title fight brought the best out of the Basildon community who united as one to support a local hero. Without doubt it helped him to achieve a life-long ambition of a world title for himself and honour for the town.

At the same time as Marsh was needing and getting local support in his title bid, another local cause was gathering momentum to raise in excess of £1 million to create a much-needed haven for cancer victims in the area, St Luke's Hospice. What started as a dream for Matron Trudy Cox in 1983, as she worked among the local sick as a district nurse, began to turn into spectacular reality as first a building formerly called Fobbing Farm was found, and then money started to roll in from every conceivable source in and around the district. Trudy's first target was a figure slightly over £400,000 but by the time this was raised inflation and other hidden expenses had frustratingly pushed up the required figure to over a million pounds.

By 1990 Basildon had united to raise a magnificent £850,000 toward the target and the project had developed into the most outstanding community effort seen so far in Basildon. In that year the hospice welcomed the first day-care patients and was officially opened by the Duchess of Norfolk on 26 September and later visited by Diana, Princess of Wales. However, before the eight rooms could open for full-time care, a great deal more money was and still is needed.

The spirit shown by local people in digging deep into their pockets to support such a worthy cause is a credit to Basildon, and a highlight in the comparatively short history of the town, as it heads towards its 50th birthday in 1999 and on into the next century.

Index

Abercrombie Plan, 48
Agricultural depression, 2
Ambulance station, 56
Amess, David, M.P., 98
Archer, Tony, 96
Archibald, William, 96
Armfield, F., 35
Arterial Road, 26, 56
Auliff, M., 50

Baggs, Cyril, 83
Balch, William, 109
Ball, Councillor Tony, 96, 108
Ballard, Councillor Peter, 96
Barstable Cottage, 72-75
Basildon: Centre, 90, 107; Development
    Corporation, 50, 52, 108, 109; District
    Council, 104; golf course, 89; Hall, 72;
    market, 77; Old Rectory, 30, 72; Sports
    Council, 87; Urban District Council, 106
Baylis, Mrs. Eve, 64
Bebington, H. E., 91
Billericay: Rural District Council, 106;
    St Andrew's Hospital, 81-2; Urban
    District Council, 48, 50, 106
Bluehouse Farm, 70
Body, Sir Richard, M.P., 97
Boniface, Charles, 50, 112
Bowers Gifford, 17, 91
Braine, Sir Bernard, M.P., 81, 97
Brewitt's Farm, 70
Brooke House, 80

Campbell: buses, 32; family, 32
Car ownership, 51
Carey's Building Supplies, 15
Carpenter, Rev. Herbert, 30
Carreras Rothmans, 87, 109
Chalvedon Hall, 72
Chapman, Terry, 96
Cheshire, Alfred, 102
Chittock family, 29
Chowdhary, Dr. Dharm, 30
Church Road, 24

Churches: All Saints, Vange, 9, 70; Gordon
    Hall Free Church, 61; Holy Cross, 9,
    24, 61, 70; St Alban's, 24; St Andrew's,
    61; St Basil's, 63; St Gabriel's, Pitsea,
    70; St Margaret's, Bowers Gifford, 24;
    St Martin-le-Tours, 63, 80, 113;
    St Michael's, Pitsea, 9, 70; St Nicholas',
    9, 41, 70 City buses, 33
Civic offices/officers, 102-6
Coker, Dame Elizabeth, 109
Collings family, 15
Community halls, 58
Coney, Stuart, 117
Cook, Herbert, 9
Cottis's bakery, 35
Cove, Bill, 63
Cox, Matron Trudy, 117
Crane, the, 56
Cranes Industrial Estate, 56, 63, 69
Crown Hotel, 86

D-Day, 45
Davies, Councillor W.H., 92
Dew, Kate and Charlie, 15
Diana, Princess of Wales, 117
Dixon, Eric, 86
Dove, Councillor Alfred, 56, 84
Drake, Alison, 117
Dunlop, Rev. Arthur, 63
Dunton, 9, 17

Eastgate International Centre, 80
Elizabeth, H.M. the Queen Mother, 113
Essex Country Club, Laindon, 86
Evelin, Ernest, 26

Felmores farm, 70
Ferrier, William, 59
Findlay, Douglas, 58
Flynn, Olly, 117
Fobbing Farm, 117
Ford, John, 91
Ford Motor Company: 70, 90, 109, 112;
    Research Centre, 70

Fortune of War, Laindon (now the *Hustlers*), 26
Foulger, Harry, 2
Frampton Farm, 70
Freeman, Bill, 113
Frierns Farm, 41
Fryerns: Area Tenants Association, 59; Boys' Club, 63; Community Centre, 87
Fullbrook, Julian, 98

Gadsdon, Mrs. Christina, 93
Gale, Lieut. Gen. Sir Humfrey, 109
Galloway, Douglas, 112
Gardner, Edward, Q.C., M.P., 97
General Elections, 97-101
Ghyllgrove housing, 66
Gibbins, Rev. Ronald, 61
Gladwin, Charlotte, 43
Gloucester, Duke and Duchess of, 113
Gloucester Park, 87
Goodfellow, Bernard, 83
Goodwin, Sir Reginald, 109
Gorman, Teresa, M.P., 100
Gower, Iris, 37
Grant, Eric, 45
Great Eastern Railway, 1
Greaves, Tony, 95
Green, L.W., 47
Gregory, Mrs. E.J., 50
Grimwood, Rev. P., 63
Gunter, Ray, M.P., 97

Harrows, the, N. Benfleet (now the *Dick Turpin*), 26
Harvey, Herbert, 91
Hatt, Alma, 48, 95, 100-1, 102-3
Haven, the, plotlands museum, 17, 20
Hawkridge, Eric and Marjorie, 54
Helmore, Thomas, 2
Henbest, Allan, 77
Hickey, Mrs. Chris, 36-7
Hillman, Dick, 33
Hollands, Stanley, 52
Holliday, Bert, 24
Holy Cross Recreation Ground, 87
Honeypot Lane, 24
Hospice, St Luke's, 117
Housing, demolition of, 75
Howard, Ebenezer, 48
Howard, Harold George, 22-4

Humm, James, 2
Hunts Farm, 70
Huxley-Jones, Adrian, 113

Illner, Johann, 43
Incendiary bombs, 41

James, Walter and Anna, 72
Jess Keir's café, 35
Jobson, F.C., J.P., 50
Jones, Councillor Clifford, 95

Kaye, Albert, 91
Keay House, 77, 93
Keay, Sir Lancelot, 50, 109
Kelting, A.O., 109
Kent, Duchess of, 113
Kiddell, Bill, 92
King, Rev. John, 61
Knapton, Brig. W.G.D., 50, 112
Knight, Mrs. W.M., 50

Lacey, George, 9
Laindon: Community Centre, 86; Hall, 72; Memorial Hall, 86; Residents' Protection Association, 50, 76
Land auctions, 2
Land Company of London, 2
Land, Matthew, 91
Langdon-Dowsett, Herbert, 52
Langdon Hills: beauty spots, 52; Sanatorium, 35, 41
Leatherland, Lord, 91
Lee Chapel North neighbourhood, 17, 66, 75-6, 87
Lerpiniere, Mrs., 15
Lewis, Charles, 102
Little Chalvedon Hall, 72
Local Government re-organisation, 104
London, Tilbury & Southend Railway Co., 1

Macpherson, Sir John, 109
Maddox, Ethel, 65
Manns, F.G.E., 83
Marchant, Edward, 92
Marconi Wireless Telegraph Company, 87, 109
Marsh, Terry, 117
Martin, Eamonn, 117

Martin, Stan and Phyllis, 54
Mawer, Air Commodore Allen, 112
Maycock, Harry, 9
McCrindle, Robert, M.P., 97
Mead, James, 9
Methodism, 59-61
Mitchinson, R.C., 96, 101, 104, 106
Moat House Farm, 70
Moonman, Eric, M.P., 97
Morgan, J.E., 95, 103
Moss, Tony, 75
Moyler, John T., 65
Muhammed Ali, 117
Mundy, Dorothy, 43
Murray, Len, 113

New Town: a case for, 48-9; Blues, 58;
    designation, 50; first tenants, 53; Master
    Plan, 51; housing, progress and statistics,
    66; Town Centre plan, 77; traffic
    segregation, 69
New Towns Act, 1946, 48
Newman, Tom, 9
Newman-Brown, Mr. and Mrs., 59-60
Norfolk, Duchess of, 117

Old Tom's Motor Services, 33
Oliphants, 30, 39, 72

Parfitt, Bill, 63
Parkinson, Cliff and Bertie, 30
Parsons, Ted, 59
Penny, Helena, 43
Philip, Prince, 113
Phillimore, Rev. Charles, 61
Pitsea: Hall, 72; *Railway Hotel*, 22, 86;
    Rectory, 32
Plotlands and plotlanders, 10
Population: statistics, 8-9; targets, 51
Post Office, 80
Potter, Councillor John, 96, 106, 108
Proctor, Harvey, M.P., 97, 98
Protheroe, E.L., 50

Raikes, Sir Victor, M.P., 97
Railway: 1, 2; station campaign, 89-90;
    stations, 1, 8
Railway Hotel, 17, 22, 26, 86
Rectory Road, 24
Redgrave Road, 53

Reed, Alderman Ernest, 35
Residents' Protection Association, 50, 69, 76
Reynolds, Rev. F.W.J., 39
Robson, V.G., 86
Rolski, Joe, 69
Ross, George, 69, 76
Rosser, John, 106
Ruggles-Brise, Sir John, 82

St Alban's Hall, 24
Sargent, Mrs. D.M., 50
Saunders, 'Doughy', 35
Schools: Barstable Grammar/Technical,
    86; Chowdhary, 30; Craylands, 86;
    Fryerns Grammar/Technical, 86;
    Laindon Park (previously St Nicholas'),
    43; Nevendon, 83; Pitsea Primary, 83;
    Swan Mead, 83; Timberlog, 86, 92;
    Vange Primary, 83; Whitmore, 83
Shannon, Dr. William, 30
Shaw, Alice, 43
Shaw, Rev. Donald, 59-61
Shops: 9, 17, 56, 77, 80; Carey's Building
    Supplies, 15; Co-op, the first, 71; Marks
    and Spencer, 80
Short, E., 26
Sibbons, George, 86
Silkin, Rt. Hon. Lewis, M.P., 50
Simmons, Maud, 43
Smith, Albert and Rose, 54
Smith, Col. S.A., 50
South-East Essex Wholesale Dairies, 56,
    108
Southfields Farm, 70
Southwood Court, 113
Spence, Sir Basil, 69, 83, 106
Stacey, Mr. and Mrs., 29
Stacey's Corner, 29
Strutt, Albert, 35
Styles family, 72
Swimming Pool, 87

Tanswell, Councillor H.E., 91
Taylor, David, 87, 95, 103
Taylor, Gladys, 56, 81
Teleflex Products, 87
Thomas, Elizabeth and Henry, 14
Thomas's Garage, 29, 30
Timberlog Lane, 24
Tinworth, Councillor H., 96, 108

Town Centre, plan, 77
Town Hall, 106
Town Manager scheme, 93, 103
Towngate Theatre, 90, 107

Unemployment peak, 109
Urban Studies paper, 1970, 8

Vange: Fire Brigade, 26; Hall, 72
Varty, Robert, 2

Wadsworth, S.A., 103
Walker, John and Betty, 53
Wartime, 8, 38-47 Wat Tyler Country
    Park, 72, 96, 113

Watson, Mr. and Mrs., 24
Webb, John, 117
Webber, Rev. Canon Lionel, 63
Webster, Tom and Dick, 33
West, Charles, 63
White's Farm, 41
Whitehead, Geoffrey, 83
Whitehead, R.E., 97
Whitmore, Lady, 54
Winfield, Rev. William, 61
Witherspoon, Tim, 117
Wolfenden, Grace, 47

Yates, Matthew, 117